PRAYER

FINDING INTIMACY WITH GOD

Leader's Resource Guide

(INCLUDES STUDY GUIDE)

LECTIO™

UNVEILING SCRIPTURE AND TRADITION

TIM GRAY

Nihil Obstat: Tomas Fuerte, S.T.L., *Censor Librorum*
Imprimatur: Most Reverend Samuel J. Aquila, S.T.L., Archbishop of Denver, December 2015

Writers: Ashley Crane, Kris Gray

Video Production: Jon Ervin, Steve Flanigan, Justin Leddick, Kevin Mallory, Ted Mast, John Schmidt

Print Production/Graphic Design: Ann Diaz, Brenda Kraft, Jane Myers, Devin Schadt

Augustine Institute
6160 South Syracuse Way, Suite 310
Greenwood Village, CO 80111

For more information: 303-937-4420
Formed.org

Printed in the United States of America
ISBN 978-0-9966768-6-1

TABLE OF CONTENTS

PRAYER:
FINDING INTIMACY WITH GOD

LECTIO™

Unveiling Scripture and Tradition

What Is LECTIO?

To read is to discover meaning from written symbols or text. Letters form into words, words into sentences, and sentences into whole paragraphs and pages that communicate our thoughts, teach new ideas, and narrate stories that we find amusing, sorrowful, imaginative, or deeply profound.

The Latin term *lectio* means "reading." The tradition of reading Sacred Scripture for prayer and reflection was practiced by many of the early Church Fathers—St. Ambrose, St. Jerome, St. Augustine, St. Cyprian, and St. John Chrysostom, just to name a few. Benedictine monks later developed this practice into the tradition known as *lectio divina*, or "divine reading."

LECTIO uses the practice of prayerful reading and study to help us dive more deeply into the truths of the faith and discover the profound meaning and purpose of Sacred Scripture, Sacred Tradition, and Church History. We combine engaging sessions led by Catholic teachers with practical guidance for living the faith and developing the disciplines of reading, reflecting, and responding.

By prayerfully reading and understanding the texts of Sacred Scripture and Tradition, we can come to discover the story of salvation into which our Baptism has united us, the history of God's people through the centuries, and the depth of God's love for each of us.

WELCOME TO LECTIO

Welcome to the *Lectio* Study Series. In these sessions of *Lectio*, you will discover the profound importance, meaning, purpose, and beauty of Sacred Scripture and Sacred Tradition, as seen through the eyes of the Church.

Lectio studies are designed for Adult Faith Formation to help unveil both Sacred Scripture and Sacred Tradition. The Latin word *lectio* means "reading," and often refers to a careful and prayerful reading of Scripture. These studies cover a wide variety of topics, including individual books or letters of the Bible, the lives and writings of the saints, Church teaching, and topics to help serve the formation of Catholics living out the call of the New Evangelization.

A LECTIO SESSION

This Study Guide takes you step by step through each session, both the small group gathering and video teaching, as well as five days of personal follow-up study. The resources are carefully crafted to lead you through an opening of your heart and mind to God's Word and the Traditions of the Catholic Church.

Here is what you will find in each LECTIO session:

CONNECT

1. **Opening Prayer:** The *Catechism of the Catholic Church* teaches that "the psalms ... teach us how to pray" (CCC 2587). For this reason we will draw our Opening Prayer for each session from a different psalm.

2. **Introduction:** We begin with a brief overview of the topic, including the key points for the session. This helps contextualize the topic, shows its relevance for daily life, and inspires you to delve into a particular aspect of the Faith.

3. **CONNECT Questions:** You'll review the memory verse and daily reflections from the previous session and then share your thoughts on questions related to the new session.

VIDEO

4. **Video Teaching:** The video segments present teaching that delves into and makes relevant the Sacred Scripture and Sacred Tradition of the Catholic Church. The video teachings for the study on prayer are presented by Dr. Tim Gray, president of Augustine Institute. An outline of each teaching is included in the Study Guide.

DISCUSS

5. **DISCUSS Questions:** Each video segment is followed by questions that will help you personalize and take ownership of the topics of the session.

6. **Memory Verse:** The psalms encourage us to treasure God's Word in our heart through memorization, saying, "I have laid up thy word in my heart..." (Psalm 119:11). You are encouraged to memorize and reflect on a Scripture verse for every session to help nurture your faith.

7. **Closing Prayer:** The Closing Prayer has been chosen to reflect back to God an appropriate response to his loving action in the session.

8. **For Further Reading:** For supplemental study, you are encouraged to refer to the additional reading resources.

9. Quotes, Tips, and Definitions: We have included throughout the study interesting quotes and excerpts from saints, Catholic documents, the *Catechism of the Catholic Church*, and Catholic authors to enhance your understanding of each topic.

COMMIT

The Study Guide includes five daily COMMIT reflections that will help you more deeply explore the main topics of each session and more firmly commit to following Christ in your daily life. These reflections include more information on Sacred Scripture and Sacred Tradition, as well as topics such as geography, history, and art. These reflections will also include times of prayer, including the practice of Scripture meditation known as *lectio divina*.

AN OVERVIEW OF LECTIO DIVINA

Lectio divina is an ancient practice of enhancing one's prayer life through the power of God's Word. The term itself means "divine reading" of the Sacred Scriptures. It is our hope that by using these simple steps each day as you study Sacred Scripture in LECTIO, you will develop an effective way to study and pray with God's Word and hear God's voice in your daily life.

- *Sacred Reading of the Scriptures (Lectio):* The reading and rereading of the Scripture passage, paying close attention to words, details, themes, and patterns that speak to you.

- *Meditation (Meditatio):* Meditating or reflecting on what you've read to gain understanding. Allow the Holy Spirit to guide you as you spend time pondering what you have read and striving to understand it in meditation.

- *Prayer (Oratio):* A time to bring your meditative thoughts to God in prayer. Speak with God about how the connections and implications of your meditation on the Scripture affect your life and the lives of those around you.

- *Contemplation (Contemplatio):* A time of quiet and rest, we listen and await God's voice. Contemplation allows one to enter decisively and more deeply into the Mystery of God – this is no small endeavor, so be patient as you engage this step and strive to be receptive to God's voice speaking into your life.

- *Resolution (Resolutio):* A call for resolution and action, inviting you to respond to God and the things you have read in Scripture and prayed about.

To learn more about *lectio divina*, refer to Dr. Tim Gray's book *Praying Scripture for a Change*, available at www.AscensionPress.com.

SESSION 1

PRAYER: AN INTIMATE DIALOGUE

OPENING PRAYER

O come, let us sing to the LORD;
let us make a joyful noise to the rock of our salvation!
Let us come into his presence with thanksgiving;
let us make a joyful noise to him with songs of praise!

For the LORD is a great God,
and a great King above all gods.
In his hand are the depths of the earth;
the heights of the mountains are his also.

The sea is his, for he made it;
for his hands formed the dry land.
O come, let us worship and bow down,
let us kneel before the Lord, our Maker!

For he is our God,
and we are the people of his pasture,
and the sheep of his hand.
Amen.

—Psalm 95:1–7

INTRODUCTION

Have you ever had an experience in prayer where you felt deeply, intimately connected to God? Have you ever felt like you were merely talking to yourself during prayer? Chances are most of us have experienced both ends of the spectrum, and no matter how healthy our prayer life, there is always room for improvement. We begin our study on prayer by exploring the importance of approaching it as a two-way conversation. Our speaking to God is one part of the conversation. Often it's the other part, God speaking to us, with which most people struggle. Does God speak to us? And if so, how do we hear him?

Saint Dominic / Gianni Dagli Orti /
The Art Archive at Art Resource, NY

CONNECT

What is your earliest memory of praying?

How would you define (or explain) prayer for someone who had never heard of it?

DISCUSS

AN ENCOUNTER WITH GOD
Watch the teaching on video. The following is a brief outline of the topics covered.

I. Prayer—An Invitation to Encounter God
   A. Benedict XVI: Christianity is not simply a creed, but rather an encounter with the living God (*Deus Caritas Est*, 1)
   B. We need to be taught how to pray (Luke 11:1)
   C. *Lectio divina* as a method of encountering God in prayer

II. The Problem of Prayer
   A. We know we "ought" to pray, but it often seems like an obligation
   B. Inconsistency of prayer in everyday life
   C. Experience of dryness and aridity in monologue prayer

III. Prayer as a Dialogue
   A. God loves us and speaks to us—he speaks
      the Word, his Son, Jesus
   B. God's normative way of speaking is through
      his Word in the Scriptures
      1. St. Ambrose: "When you pick up the
         Scriptures, God speaks to you"
      2. St. Cyprian: "When you hear God in his
         Word, he speaks to you"
      3. St. Augustine hears "*tolle lege*"
         (take and read), reads Romans 13:11–14,
         and hears God speaking directly to him
   C. To whom is God's Word in Scripture addressed?
      1. Historically, God speaks to Abraham, Moses,
         Mary, Peter, etc.
      2. The secret of the saints is that they hear God's
         Word in Scripture as addressed to them
         in the present
      3. We need to come and listen to God; we
         need to "take and read" so that there can
         be a dynamic dialogue with God
      4. Prayer is God's thirst for us (CCC 2560)

DISCUSS

1. What was one thing you heard for the first time or that was an "aha" moment for you?

_____

_____

_____

2. What obstacles to prayer do you experience? How have you dealt with these in the past?
How might approaching prayer as an encounter and a dialogue affect your experience?

_____

_____

_____

3. Do you feel it is easy or difficult to hear God speaking directly to you in Scripture? Why?

_____

_____

_____

MEMORY VERSE

"I will seek him whom my soul loves."
—**Song of Solomon 3:2**

CLOSING PRAYER

Heavenly Father,
thank you for calling us to intimate conversation
with you in prayer.
Give us the strength and the perseverance
to continually work to overcome all obstacles
to prayer in our lives.
Teach us to listen as you speak to us in the Scriptures.
Guide us into an ever-deepening love for you.
We ask this in the name of your Son,
our Lord Jesus Christ. Amen.

Saint Francis of Sales / © RMN-Grand Palais / Art Resource, NY

FOR FURTHER READING

**Tim Gray, "Introduction: The Problem of Prayer" and "Chapter 1: The Secret of the Saints"
in *Praying Scripture for a Change* (Ascension Press, 2009)**

***Catechism of the Catholic Church* on Prayer, paragraphs 2558–2696**

"Pray constantly." —1 Thessalonians 5:17

Scripture has a lot to say about prayer. Almost anywhere you turn in the Bible you will find: someone praying; instructions for where, when, and how to pray; accounts of God answering prayer; psalms praising God for his answers to prayer; prophets scolding God's people for not praying; etc. Prayer is everywhere in Scripture, and St. Paul's instructions to the Thessalonians—and to us—sum up the biblical attitude as concisely as possible: pray constantly!

"For me, prayer is an aspiration of the heart, it is a simple glance directed to heaven, it is a cry of gratitude and love in the midst of trial as well as joy; finally it is something great, supernatural, which expands my soul and unites me to Jesus."
—St. Therese of Lisieux

The story of salvation begins with God creating mankind for union with himself. That union is destroyed by sin, but no matter how great the distance between God and man, "God tirelessly calls each person to that mysterious encounter known as prayer" (CCC 2567). God wrote this call to prayer into the very structure of time from the beginning when he blessed the seventh day and established it as a day of rest and worship (see Genesis 2:2–3 and Exodus 20:8–10).

How do you keep Sunday, the Lord's Day, as a day of prayer? How does this influence the rest of your week?

_____

_____

To keep his people close to him, God gave the Israelites detailed instructions on when and how to encounter him in prayer. Two pillars in the life of prayer for God's people in the Old Covenant were Israel's annual liturgical feasts and the Book of Psalms. The liturgical feasts provided a rhythm of prayer corresponding to the changing seasons and were rooted in God's saving actions in Israel's history. The structure and repetition of the feasts brought Israel together in prayer as a community. The Book of Psalms was the prayer book of Israel, essential not only to the annual feasts and the Temple liturgy, but also to the prayers of the family and individual at home. God's laws regarding prayer and worship, where the initiative of God's mighty deeds for his people were recalled and his people responded with praise, are a reminder that prayer is a dialogue—God starts the conversation, and we respond.

Look up the following psalms: Psalm 73:28 and 105:1–4. Take a moment to recall and praise God for his many works in your own life.

_____

_____

_____

In the New Testament we see the ultimate example of prayer in the life of Christ. Jesus often takes the time to go off on his own for prayer. He prays with and for his disciples. And he gives us the most explicit instruction concerning how to pray in the Our Father (Matthew 6:9–13).

Prayer in the Garden of Gethsemane / Scala / Art Resource, NY

After his death and resurrection, Jesus' disciples continued to practice what the Master had taught. In the early Church we find prayer as an important pillar of the Christian life: "And they devoted themselves to the apostles' teaching and fellowship, to the breaking of the bread and the prayers" (Acts 2:42). Prayer, both communal and individual, has always been a necessary part of life for the people of God, under both the Old and New Covenants.

What does your life of prayer have in common with prayer as lived throughout Salvation History?

_____

_____

_____

COMMIT—DAY 2
THE PROBLEM OF PRAYER

What are some activities you know to be good and important, but that you simply don't like to do—the ones that always seem to get moved to the bottom of your "to do" list?

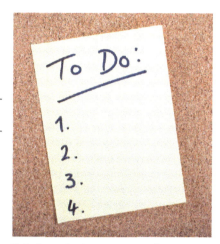

_____

_____

Whether it's going to the dentist or folding laundry or cleaning the gutters, we each have our own list of chores and duties that are important, but not particularly enjoyable. If prayer has ever made an appearance on this list for you, don't worry—you're not alone!

To Do List © chrisdorney / shutterstock.com

We all know that prayer is a necessary and important component of our spiritual health, but it doesn't always seem like it's working. Prayer appears throughout the Scriptures, but for many of us, prayer doesn't come easily. We often feel like we are just going through the motions but not accomplishing anything. Or sometimes we feel like it is a one-sided conversation—we show up but God doesn't. It's hard to keep doing something faithfully when we aren't seeing results!

What is your greatest struggle with prayer right now?

_____

_____

_____

The problem of prayer is nothing new—Jesus' own disciples asked him to teach them how to pray (see Luke 11:1), and St. Paul lamented that "we do not know how to pray as we ought" (Romans 8:26). In our modern world, we face a particular stumbling block to fruitful prayer. We live in a culture that has done its best to completely eliminate silence and stillness from our daily experience. We are constantly bombarded with images, sounds, and ideas. It's impossible to read an article on the Internet without a pop-up ad interrupting us before we have finished. We have been conditioned to constantly move from one piece of information to the next, without completing anything. In fact, a recent study found that the average person in our technology-saturated society has an attention span that is literally shorter than that of a goldfish: only eight seconds for humans, compared to nine seconds for goldfish.

This combination of constant distraction and an ever-shortening attention span makes it difficult to be quiet long enough to even start prayer, let alone enter into a true dialogue. In the midst of all the noise surrounding and filling us, we might be able to speak the first words in our conversation of prayer, but it is certainly not so easy to listen for a response. And so often, when God doesn't respond immediately, we quit. Listening to God in prayer requires patience—a patient willingness to sit with God in silence in order to hear.

In one of his encounters with God, the prophet Elijah also had to wade through a lot of noise and distraction to hear God.

> *"And behold, the LORD passed by, and a great and strong wind rent the mountains, and broke in pieces the rocks before the LORD, but the LORD was not in the wind; and after the wind an earthquake, but the LORD was not in the earthquake; and after the earthquake a fire, but the LORD was not in the fire; and after the fire a still small voice. And when Elijah heard it, he wrapped his face in his mantle and went out and stood at the entrance of the cave."*
>
> —1 Kings 19:11b–13a

Disposing ourselves to listen for that still small voice is a habit that requires practice and patience. Not only do we need to create a quiet external environment in which to pray, but we also have to learn to cultivate internal silence. The room we're in might be so quiet we could hear a pin drop, but can we hear God speaking to us over the sound of our own thoughts?

What are some things you can do to cultivate a habit of exterior and interior silence, and practice the art of patient listening?

_____

_____

Put it into practice. Psalm 46:10 says, "Be still, and know that I am God." When Elijah heard the still small voice, he "went out and stood at the entrance of the cave" and waited. Hear God speak in the passage of 1 Kings above, or in Psalm 46:10, and now take time to sit in silence before the Lord. Can you make it 5 minutes?

"Never be in a hurry; do everything quietly and in a calm spirit. Do not lose your inner peace for anything whatsoever, even if your whole world seems upset."

—St. Francis de Sales

Sunset at Jakes landing © Vadim.Petrov / shutterstock.com

COMMIT—DAY 3
LECTIO: "I THIRST"

The *Catechism* tells us that God thirsts for a relationship with us, and that prayer is our response to this thirst (CCC 2560–61). Today's *lectio divina* explores Jesus' declaration of thirst during his crucifixion. Christ's cry from the cross, "I thirst," expresses a reality beyond the physical torment of crucifixion and communicates a deep desire, a desire that is only quenched when each of us personally responds to Jesus.

> **LECTIO:** The practice of praying with Scripture, *lectio divina*, begins with an active and close reading of the Scripture passage. Read the verse below and then answer the questions to take a closer look at some of the details of the passage.

"After this Jesus, knowing that all was now finished, said (to fulfil the Scripture), 'I thirst.' A bowl full of vinegar stood there; so they put a sponge full of the vinegar on hyssop and held it to his mouth. When Jesus had received the vinegar, he said, 'It is finished'; and he bowed his head and gave up his spirit.

Since it was the day of Preparation, in order to prevent the bodies from remaining on the cross on the sabbath (for that sabbath was a high day), the Jews asked Pilate that their legs might be broken, and that they might be taken away. So the soldiers came and broke the legs of the first, and of the other who had been crucified with him; but when they came to Jesus and saw that he was already dead, they did not break his legs. But one of the soldiers pierced his side with a spear, and at once there came out blood and water. He who saw it has borne witness— his testimony is true, and he knows that he tells the truth—that you also may believe."

—John 19:28–35

What need or desire does Jesus express in this passage? What does he receive?

_____

_____

What does Jesus give in this passage?

_____

_____

What reason does St. John offer for presenting his testimony in this passage?

_____

_____

> **MEDITATIO:** *Lectio*, a close reading and rereading, is followed by *meditatio*, time to reflect on the Scripture passage and to ponder the reason for particular events, descriptions, details, phrases, and even echoes from other Scripture passages that were noticed during *lectio*. Take some time now to meditate on the verse from page 11.

The following meditation on Jesus' thirst for each one of us is attributed to Mother Teresa and was read by Father John Riccardo on "Christ is the Answer" on Ave Maria Radio: https://avemariaradio.net/wp-content/uploads/2013/03/Jesus-I-Thirst.pdf

Mother Teresa statue in Prem Dan house, Kolkata
© *Zvonimir Atletic / shutterstock.com*

"I Thirst for You. Yes, that is the only way to even begin to describe My love for you. I THIRST FOR YOU. I thirst to love you and to be loved by you—that is how precious you are to Me. I THIRST FOR YOU. Come to Me, and I will fill your heart and heal your wounds. I will make you a new creation, and give you peace, even in all your trials I THIRST FOR YOU. You must never doubt My mercy, My acceptance of you, My desire to forgive, My longing to bless you and live My life in you. I THIRST FOR YOU. If you feel unimportant in the eyes of the world, that matters not at all. For Me, there is no one any more important in the entire world than you. I THIRST FOR YOU. Open to Me, come to Me, thirst for Me, give me your life—and I will prove to you how important you are to My Heart."
                                        —Blessed Teresa of Calcutta

From the cross Jesus said, "I thirst," and in response he was given vinegar or sour wine—a common drink of the lower classes that, although cheap, was considered refreshing. What does Christ thirst for from you? What can you offer him on a daily basis? Weekly? Over the course of your whole life?

_____

_____

The *Catechism* states: "Whether we realize it or not, prayer is the encounter of God's thirst with ours. God thirsts that we may thirst for him. . . . Prayer is . . . a response of love to the thirst of the only Son of God" (CCC 2560–61). Why is it important to understand prayer as a response to God rather than something we initiate? What effect might this view have on your prayer life?

_____

_____

In John 19:28–35, Christ thirsts for us, but we cannot even respond to him in prayer without his help. From the cross Jesus gives up his Spirit (verse 30) and blood and water flow from his pierced side (verse 34). How do the Holy Spirit and the life of the Church (symbolized by the blood and the water) enable us to respond to God in prayer?

_____

_____

> **ORATIO, CONTEMPLATIO, RESOLUTIO:** Having read and meditated on today's Scripture passage, take some time to bring your thoughts to God (*oratio*) and engage God in silence (*contemplatio*). Then end your prayer by making a simple concrete resolution (*resolutio*) to respond to God's prompting of your heart in today's prayer.

_____

_____

_____

Crucifixion from manuscript Book of Prayers of Jeanne de Laval, Queen of Naples / Gianni Dagli Orti / The Art Archive at Art Resource, NY

COMMIT—DAY 4
GOD SPEAKS

Old open Bible © Manczurov / shutterstock.com

Do you know someone who claims to have heard God speak to him or her? Maybe you have experienced God speaking to you. Because prayer is meant to be a dialogue, not a monologue, we can trust that God will speak to us. Even so, it's not typical to hear a voice from a burning bush or an angel bearing a message or even the still small voice that Elijah heard. As much as a big booming voice from heaven might make prayer easier, that's not God's normal way of communicating. So how are we supposed to hear God speak to us? God speaks to us primarily through his Word in the Scriptures.

> *"Prayer purifies us, reading instructs us. . . . If one wants to be always in God's company, he must pray regularly and read regularly. When we pray, we talk to God; when we read, God talks to us."*
> —St. Isidore of Seville

At first it may seem like a bit of a stretch to take words written thousands of years ago for a particular audience, in a specific time and place, and read them as being addressed to each of us personally. But God's living Word is big enough for everybody—it is just as relevant and personal for each of us today as it was for the authors and the original audiences for whom it was originally written.

Is there a Scripture verse that is particularly meaningful or applicable to your life right now? (It might be something you have memorized, something you heard or read recently, or even something that made an impression, but you can't remember the exact verse.)

_____

_____

The Church has always recognized both a literal and spiritual sense (meaning) in the words of the Bible. One passage often has multiple layers of meaning—the literal sense of the words, the way the passage points forward to Jesus, the way it applies to each of us individually, and the truth it teaches about eternity (see CCC 115–119 for more on the senses of Scripture). Thus it is possible, for example, to recognize that while Jesus' direction to St. Peter to "put out into the deep" (Luke 5:4) was a direction for St. Peter to literally put his boat deeper in the water of the Sea of Galilee for a catch of fish, we might also hear Jesus speak those words to our own heart as a call to enter into a deeper relationship with him in our own life.

St. Paul wrote to his disciple Timothy, "All scripture is inspired by God and profitable for teaching, for reproof, for correction, and for training in righteousness, that the man of God may be complete, equipped for every good work" (2 Timothy 3:16–17). This doesn't mean that our common approach to Scripture should be to flip through the Bible as if it were a divine Magic 8 Ball™ and expect to quickly get an answer for any question. God can direct or speak to us in this way, just as he directed St. Augustine to "take and read," and St. Augustine's heart was moved as he read Romans 13:13–14. However, while this method of opening the Bible to a random page and taking the first verse we see as God's response to whatever is on our mind might produce helpful results at times, at other times we might unexpectedly get an answer about how to properly butcher our sacrificial goat from the Book of Leviticus or a lengthy royal genealogy from 2nd Chronicles.

Just as finding silence for prayer takes practice, prayerfully reading Scripture is a habit that also takes time and effort to establish. A habit of praying with Scripture gives God the opportunity to talk to us and allows us to learn how to listen. This is the secret of the saints: immerse yourself in God's Word knowing it is addressed to you, and you will hear God speak to you.

> *"Let them remember, however, that prayer should accompany the reading of Sacred Scripture, so that a dialogue takes place between God and man. For 'we speak to him when we pray; we listen to him when we read the divine oracles.'"* —CCC 2653 (Quoting St. Ambrose)

Consider your current habits for reading Scripture. Do you read the Bible on a regular basis? Is it for prayer or for study? What are some steps you can take this week to begin praying with Scripture or to increase the time you spend praying with Scripture?

_____

_____

Hands and Rosary © Kzenon / shutterstock.com

Fra Angelico, *Annunciation,* c. 1450, Convent of San Marco, Florence

The Annunciation / Erich Lessing / Art Resource, NY

Fra Angelico was a Dominican friar and early Italian Renaissance painter devoted exclusively to religious art. The 16th-century biographer Vasari said of him, "It is impossible to bestow too much praise on this holy father, who was so humble and modest in all that he did and said and whose pictures were painted with such facility and piety." Fra Angelico was beatified by Pope St. John Paul II in 1982 and is a patron saint of Catholic artists.

Fra Angelico was among the Dominican friars who moved into Florence's newly rebuilt friary of San Marco. There, in addition to his responsibilities as a friar, he set about the task of decorating the convent, painting some forty frescoes in the individual cells, as well as several paintings in corridors and communal areas. The above *Annunciation* fresco can still be seen where Fra Angelico first painted it, at the top of the staircase leading to the dormitory level of the north corridor of one of the cloisters. Light from an east-facing window in the corridor bathes the painting in the early morning hours, highlighting its colors, and the window's location intensifies this effect in the early spring, in particular around the March 25th feast of the Annunciation. Fra Angelico sets his *Annunciation* scene under an arched portico, similar to those that encircle the cloister's ground floor garden area. The painting's garden is populated with small white flowers, and just beyond the simple fence are Tuscan cypresses. The linear perspective draws us into the picture, and its vanishing point of the small window in the cell just beyond the Annunciation scene highlights the painting's setting. With its position along the corridor's south wall, the fresco acts as an illusionary window looking out onto the garden area and thus brings the sacred scene of the Annunciation into the physical reality of the convent. In viewing the fresco, one could expect to walk directly out into the garden and find Mary and Gabriel in conversation.

This *Annunciation* is simple, and almost austere. Mary sits on a simple wooden bench. There are no images of God the Father overlooking the scene, or of the Holy Spirit preparing to descend and overshadow Mary once she has uttered her *fiat*, her "yes." There are no symbolic objects, such as lilies denoting Mary's purity. There is nothing "extra" to distract our attention from focusing solely on Mary and the angel who has come to her on God's behalf.

Look up Luke 1:26–38. In this conversation between God (through his messenger Gabriel) and Mary, who initiates? Is this a monologue, or a dialogue? How does Mary's interaction with Gabriel change over the course of the conversation?

_____

_____

_____

Both Mary and the angel take a stance of humility, with arms folded over their chests. Gabriel bends his knee and bows before the virgin, marveling at her who he is able to address as "full of grace." Mary does not bow as much as she looks directly in the face of this heavenly messenger. St. Luke tells us that she "considered in her mind" Gabriel's greeting (Luke 1:29). As the angel continues his message, Mary interjects to ask questions, to inquire and better understand God's word to her. The angel responds, giving greater understanding and also greater assurance by announcing what has already miraculously happened to Elizabeth. As Mary is able to consider, inquire, take in, and understand God's word and will, she then responds both in word and in deed, departing in haste to the hill country of Judah to serve Elizabeth (see Luke 1:38–40).

St. John Paul II, specifically noting Fra Angelico's *Annunciation*, reflected that Mary "represents the model of the Church at prayer. In all probability Mary was absorbed in prayer when the angel Gabriel came to her house in Nazareth and greeted her. This prayerful setting certainly supported the Blessed Virgin in her reply to the angel and in her generous assent to the mystery of the Incarnation. . . . We could add that for the People of God, Mary represents the model of every expression of their prayer life. In particular, she teaches Christians how to turn to God to ask for his help and support in the various circumstances of life" (General Audience, Sept. 10, 1977).

As Fra Angelico's fellow friars passed by this *Annunciation* everyday, it certainly must have assisted them to follow Mary's example in their own life of prayer. By painting the *Annunciation* as though it were taking place in the garden and portico of the cloister, the artist created a simple but beautiful reminder that God desires to step into our lives—not only his fellow friars but each of us today—and encounter us in prayer.

Take a moment to journal your ideas, questions, or insights about this lesson. Write down thoughts you had that may not have been mentioned in the text or the discussion questions. List any personal applications you got from the lessons. What challenged you the most in the teachings? How might you turn what you've learned into specific action?

_____

_____

_____

_____

_____

_____

_____

_____

_____

_____

_____

_____

_____

_____

_____

_____

_____

_____

SESSION 2

GUIGO'S LADDER: A WAY OF ASCENT

OPENING PRAYER

How can a young man keep his way pure?
By guarding it according to thy word.
With my whole heart I seek thee;
let me not wander from thy commandments!

I have laid up thy word in my heart,
that I might not sin against thee.
Blessed be thou, O Lord;
teach me thy statutes!

With my lips I declare
all the ordinances of thy mouth.
In the way of thy testimonies I delight
as much as in all riches.

I will meditate on thy precepts,
and fix my eyes on thy ways.
I will delight in thy statutes;
I will not forget thy word.
Amen.

—Psalm 119:9–16

INTRODUCTION

"For everything there is a season, and a time for every matter under heaven" (Ecclesiastes 3:1). These well-known words from the book of Ecclesiastes have found their way into all sorts of places, from greeting cards to 1960s folk rock hits. The divine ordering of things is a truth that strikes a deep chord within us, no matter how much we like to be in control. This divine order is especially important when it comes to the divine encounter of prayer. As the author of Ecclesiastes continues in verse 7, there is "a time to keep silence, and a time to speak." In the last session we were reminded that prayer is supposed to be a dialogue. In this session we will examine the specific order to this dialogue, from God initiating the conversation through the stages of our response.

CONNECT

Think of a time you felt incredibly thirsty. What quenched your thirst and refreshed you? Describe the experience.

How do you show others that you are listening attentively to them?

DISCUSS

THE LADDER OF PRAYER
Watch the teaching on video. The following is a brief outline of the topics covered.

I. Order of Prayer—God Speaks First
  A. Two ingredients—Word of God and our response _____
  B. Woman at the well (John 4:1–43)—Jesus
     speaks first, "Give me a drink" _____
  C. *Shema* (Deuteronomy 6:4–5)
     "Hear, O Israel . . ."—Israel is to listen _____
  D. Prayer requires a disposition of humility;
     the posture of a beggar _____
  E. God's complaint to Israel is that
     they didn't listen _____
  F. "You would have asked . . . [for] living water"
     (John 4:10) _____

    1. God is the fountain of living waters
      (Jeremiah 2:13)
    2. God's people chose broken, dry cisterns
    3. Samaritan woman leaves her water jar
      because she has found the living water
      in Jesus
  G. Order matters—God speaks first in the
     Scriptures, and then we respond

II. Guigo the Carthusian
  A. *Lectio*—reading
  B. *Meditatio*—meditation
  C. *Oratio*—talking to God
  D. *Contemplatio*—being with God

III. The Ladder of Prayer
  A. We have to start at the first rung
  B. "This ladder has few rungs, and yet its length
    is immense and wonderful, for its lower end
    rests upon the earth, but its top pierces the
    clouds and touches the heavens."
                —Guigo the Carthusian

DISCUSS

1. What was one thing you heard for the first time or that was an "aha" moment for you?

_____

_____

2. How does the account of the Samaritan woman at the well model an encounter with Christ in prayer? How do you relate to this account?

_____

_____

3. Have you ever tried to go straight to the top of the ladder of prayer without making use of the different rungs? Did it work? Do you feel the rungs are evenly spaced (equally easy or difficult to move between each step), or is there one step on the ladder that is particularly hard for you? Why?

_____

_____

MEMORY VERSE

"Jesus answered her, 'If you knew the gift of God, and who it is that is saying to you, "Give me a drink," you would have asked him, and he would have given you living water.'"

—**John 4:10**

CLOSING PRAYER

Lord Jesus Christ, you continually invite us
into a deeper encounter with you.
May we always respond eagerly
to your invitation.
As we receive from you
the gift of living water in prayer,
may our hearts and our lives
be transformed to reflect your glory.
Amen.

Christ and the Samaritan Woman at the Well / Erich Lessing / Art Resource, NY

FOR FURTHER READING

Tim Gray, "Chapter 2: Lectio Divina: Stairway to Heaven" in *Praying Scripture for a Change*
(Ascension Press, 2009)

Guigo the Carthusian, *Guigo II: Ladder of Monks and Twelve Meditations*
(Cistercian Publications, 1979)

COMMIT—DAY 1
HEAR, O ISRAEL

The most important prayer in the Jewish faith begins not with a supplication directed at God, but with a command for his people: "Hear, O Israel"—in Hebrew, *"Shema Yisrael."*

> *"Hear, O Israel: The LORD our God is one LORD; and you shall love the LORD your God with all your heart, and with all your soul, and with all your might."*
> —Deuteronomy 6:4–5

Mezuzah © leospek / shutterstock.com

Following Moses' instructions in Deuteronomy 6:6–9, the *Shema* was the first prayer an Israelite child learned and the last prayer breathed as one approached death. The words of the *Shema* were the first syllables spoken at morning's dawn and the last uttered before closing one's eyes for sleep. Even today the words of the *Shema* are written on a small scroll and affixed to the doorpost of a Jewish home so that they can be recalled as one comes in and goes out. These words are even worn in small boxes or phylacteries on the arms and foreheads of Orthodox Jews. This prayer was, and continues to be, the foundational prayer of the Jewish faith. Rather than asking anything of God, it is a reminder to God's people to *listen*.

This call of the *Shema* to "listen" reminds us that God is the one who initiates the conversation of prayer. We can expect to encounter God in prayer because he comes looking for us and starts the dialogue, just as he did in the very beginning when he walked in the Garden of Eden looking for Adam and Eve and asking, "Where are you?" (Genesis 3:8–9). Just as he did when he set the burning bush ablaze, attracting Moses' attention and calling his name, "Moses, Moses!" (Exodus 3:2–4). And just as he did when he woke Samuel in the middle of the night calling, "Samuel! Samuel!" (1 Samuel 3:3–4).

The prophet Samuel, whose name literally means "he who hears/listens to God" (*shema-el* = Samuel), is an important model for us as we redirect our understanding that in prayer God speaks first. Several times God called to Samuel, but Samuel did not recognize God's voice. How often is that our experience? We sit down to prayer and our assumptions about what should happen next keep us from hearing God.

Finally, Samuel is given the direction he needs—he is told to listen. Eli tells Samuel to respond, "Speak, LORD, for thy servant hears" (1 Samuel 3:9). Several times Samuel had responded, "Here I am," but it is when he stops to listen that he finally hears and recognizes God's voice. We must be persistent in our prayer, because like Samuel it may take some time for us to recognize God's voice. But in our persistence, we must not only show up, we must also listen.

We don't have to figure out how to make prayer happen—God is reaching out to us. This is precisely the model we find in the encounter between Jesus and the Samaritan woman at the well in John 4. When the Samaritan woman approached the well, Jesus was already at the well waiting for her. And in that encounter, Jesus speaks the first words: "Give me a drink" (John 4:7). The Samaritan woman seems startled by Jesus' initiation of the dialogue, saying, "How is it that you, a Jew, ask a drink of me, a woman of Samaria?" (John 4:9). We often share her surprise. Her question is often our question, too: "How is it that the God of the universe would speak into my life, into my day-to-day circumstances?" But this is exactly what God desires to do, if we would but listen.

God won't let anything get in the way of drawing close to us in prayer. What is getting in your way of listening and responding?

_____

_____

_____

Always Listen First (ALF) © Christin Chan / shutterstock.com

COMMIT—DAY 2
LIVING WATER

Early on in his conversation with the Samaritan woman at the well, Jesus draws her attention away from her material needs and opens her eyes to her deeper spiritual needs. Jesus challenges: "If you knew the gift of God, and who it is that is saying to you, 'Give me a drink,' you would have asked him and he would have given you living water" (John 4:10). In the heat of the day, the Samaritan woman comes to draw water, but her physical thirst betrays a deeper spiritual thirst that she would rather overlook—a spiritual thirst, which only God can heal and quench.

Look up the following passages: Psalm 65:9; Isaiah 12:3; Isaiah 44:3; Revelation 21:6; Revelation 22:1–2. What do these passages have in common? Why do you think Scripture uses water as an image of God?

_____

_____

_____

The Old Testament prophet Jeremiah records God's lament over the unfaithfulness of his people, Israel: "For my people have committed two evils: they have forsaken me, the fountain of living waters, and hewed out cisterns for themselves, broken cisterns, that can hold no water" (Jeremiah 2:13). The people had forsaken God and his law. They had "changed their glory for that which does not profit" (2:11) and were worshipping false gods and not living according to God's ways.

Water Flowing over Creek Rocks © Artistic Eye / shutterstock.com

The contrast between living water and broken cisterns is stark. God identifies himself as "the fountain of living waters"—a flowing spring of fresh water, never running dry. The words call up an image of cool, refreshing waters, of an oasis, of a fount that brings about and sustains abundant life wherever it flows. On the other hand, the water in a cistern is not fresh. It is rainwater that has been collected and stored for an indefinite period of time. The water is stagnant rather than flowing, and the supply is not continually replenished. And if the cistern's protective coating cracks, the water will seep out, leaving the cistern dry and empty.

In our own lives, we too are often guilty of trying to replace the living water of God with cisterns of our own making. We build broken cisterns and cling to our meager supply of stagnant water rather than trusting "the gift of God" (John 4:10). Like the Samaritan woman, we prefer to direct the conversation of prayer to stay simply on a superficial level, afraid to let God's living water into the depths of our heart. But Jesus challenges us: "If you but knew . . ." If we are used to thinking of prayer as being on our own terms, we may find the shift to seeing

God as the initiator, and ourselves as the respondents, to be less comfortable or convenient. As he leads our prayer, God will open our eyes to those areas of brokenness and sin, not to condemn us, but to set us free for a fuller relationship with him. But we must be willing to let him lead—and we must listen and follow him.

Prayer isn't always going to go as expected—just as the Samaritan woman didn't expect to meet Jesus at the well, or for him to tell her "all that I ever did." Prayer is almost guaranteed to be inconvenient sometimes, and it may even be uncomfortable. But it is always worth it! In prayer God continues to pour out on us the abundant gift of his Spirit. Like living water the Holy Spirit is life-giving and refreshing, enabling us to thrive, not just survive.

Droplet falling in blue water © Nejron Photo / shutterstock.com

Jesus promises to satisfy the thirst of those who come to him.

> *"If any one thirst, let him come to me and drink. He who believes in me, as the scripture has said, 'Out of his heart shall flow rivers of living water.'"*
>   —John 7:37b–38

When it comes to prayer, are you actively seeking to receive God's free gift, or do you build your own cistern? Do you try to make fruitful prayer happen on your own, or do you let God lead? How can you be more aware of prayer as a gift from God?

_____

_____

_____

COMMIT–DAY 3
LECTIO: JESUS AND THE SAMARITAN WOMAN

The encounter between Jesus and the Samaritan woman at the well tells us a great deal about what prayer is supposed to be. Jesus shows his love and concern in reaching out to this woman, and he demonstrates God's incredible generosity in the precious gift that he offers her. Each of us is invited to this same encounter. Jesus is waiting to speak to each of us and to satisfy our thirst with the living water of his Spirit.

> **LECTIO:** The practice of praying with Scripture, *lectio divina*, begins with an active and close reading of the Scripture passage. Read the verse below and then answer the questions to take a closer look at some of the details of the passage.

"He left Judea and departed again to Galilee. He had to pass through Samaria. So he came to a city of Samaria, called Sychar, near the field that Jacob gave to his son Joseph. Jacob's well was there, and so Jesus, wearied as he was with his journey, sat down beside the well. It was about the sixth hour.

"There came a woman of Samaria to draw water. Jesus said to her, 'Give me a drink.' For his disciples had gone away into the city to buy food. The Samaritan woman said to him, 'How is it that you, a Jew, ask a drink of me, a woman of Samaria?' For Jews have no dealings with Samaritans. Jesus answered her, 'If you knew the gift of God, and who it is that is saying to you, 'Give me a drink,' you would have asked him and he would have given you living water.' The woman said to him, 'Sir, you have nothing to draw with, and the well is deep; where do you get that living water? Are you greater than our father Jacob, who gave us the well, and drank from it himself, and his sons, and his cattle?' Jesus said to her, 'Every one who drinks of this water will thirst again, but whoever drinks of the water that I shall give him will never thirst; the water that I shall give him will become in him a spring of water welling up to eternal life.'"

—John 4:3–14

How many times are "Samaria" and "Samaritans" mentioned in this passage?

_____

_____

How many references are there to thirst or drinking or water in this passage?

_____

_____

What does the physical setting of this encounter tell you about how Jesus was likely feeling? The Samaritan woman?

_____

_____

> **MEDITATIO:** *Lectio*, a close reading and rereading, is followed by *meditatio*, time to reflect on the Scripture passage and to ponder the reason for particular events, descriptions, details, phrases, and even echoes from other Scripture passages that were noticed during *lectio*. Take some time now to meditate on the verse from page 27.

Jesus was in Jerusalem for the Passover. While there, he drove the moneychangers and those selling animals for sacrifice out of the Temple—the people responsible for caring for the Temple, God's house, were treating it as a house of trade rather than a house of prayer. The noise and concerns of this world had invaded the sacred space of encounter between God and his people.

As he left Jerusalem to return to Galilee, Jesus passed through Samaria. This was not a necessity of geography: a Jew would normally avoid Samaria when traveling between Judea and Galilee. But Jesus was going about his Father's business, and God's divine plan was that Jesus be at Jacob's well at Sychar in order to encounter a Samaritan woman in need of his gift of living water.

We let so many different things get in the way of our encounter with God in prayer. But God will stop at nothing to make himself available to us. He is waiting at the well, ready to quench our thirst with his living water.

Why is the Samaritan woman surprised that Jesus asks her for a drink? What does Jesus' willingness to talk to this woman and St. John's comment on the "necessity" of Jesus passing through Samaria teach us about prayer?

_____

_____

What is unique about the water that Jesus offers? What do you think it means to never thirst after receiving the living water?

_____

_____

Jesus tells the Samaritan woman that she would respond differently if she knew who it is that is speaking to her (verse 10). When you pray, are you mindful of "who it is" that is speaking to you? What difference does it make to approach prayer with humility and reverence rather than as something casual and routine?

_____

_____

> **ORATIO, CONTEMPLATIO, RESOLUTIO:** Having read and meditated on today's Scripture passage, take some time to bring your thoughts to God (*oratio*) and engage God in silence (*contemplatio*). Then end your prayer by making a simple concrete resolution (*resolutio*) to respond to God's prompting of your heart in today's prayer.

_____

_____

_____

Jacob's Well, Holy Land © *Augustine Institute photo. All rights reserved.*

Commit—Day 4
Guigo and the Ladder of Prayer

We have established that prayer is a conversation, and so it must have two parts: listening and responding. But even this only offers minimal guidance. How do we listen to God? How do we respond? How do we progress and grow in prayer? What is the goal of the conversation?

The Church offers us an answer to this in the ancient tradition of *lectio divina* in which, as the *Catechism* says, "The Word of God is so read and meditated that it becomes prayer" (CCC 1177). For nearly a millennia *lectio divina* has been practiced according to the four simple steps of Guigo's ladder.

Carthusian Monastery / Erich Lessing / Art Resource, NY

Guigo II was a Carthusian monk in the twelfth century. He was the ninth prior of the Grande Chartreuse monastery, the famous Carthusian motherhouse north of the city of Grenoble in the French Alps. The Grande Chartreuse was the subject of the acclaimed 2005 documentary *Into Great Silence*. Guigo is best known for his classic work on prayer, *Ladder of Monks*, in which he lays out four simple steps for praying with Scripture.

The first rung of the ladder is *lectio*, or "reading." God initiates the encounter with us, and so prayer begins with his Word. *Lectio* requires a careful reading of Scripture, paying close attention to patterns, repetition, key words, and other details of the chosen passage. This careful reading helps us to hear God's initiating dialogue. This first step introduces the topic of our conversation with God.

> *"How sweet are your words to my taste, sweeter than honey to my mouth!"*
> —Psalm 119:103

The second rung is *meditatio*, or "meditation." In this step we listen to what God is saying in the Scripture passage we read in *lectio*. We reflect on the words of the passage in order to understand what they mean. This provides the material for our conversation and guides us into our response.

> "His delight is in the law of the LORD, and on his law he meditates day and night"
> —Psalm 1:2

Oratio, or "prayer," is the third rung of the ladder. After reading and meditation, we respond to God. We often think of this step—pouring out our hearts to God—as being the whole of prayer. But it is no accident that *oratio* comes only after hearing and reflecting on what God has said. First we listen and seek to understand; then we speak.

> "Trust in him at all times, O people; pour out your heart before him; God is a refuge for us."
> —Psalm 62:8

The fourth and final rung is *contemplatio*, or "contemplation." We cannot accomplish anything in prayer apart from God, and contemplation is a special gift. The first three steps prepare us for this gift in which we are able to rest in God's presence and experience the joy and peace that come from him.

> "That I may dwell in the house of the LORD all the days of my life, to behold the beauty of the LORD."
> —Psalm 27:4

When tempted by Satan in the wilderness, Jesus replied: "Man shall not live by bread alone, but by every word that proceeds from the mouth of God" (Matthew 4:4, quoting Deuteronomy 8:3). The psalmist sings, "Your word is a lamp to my feet and a light to my path" (119:105). Why must the ladder of prayer begin with Scripture? How might the practice of praying with Scripture help you to fulfill St. Paul's exhortation to "pray constantly" (1 Thessalonians 5:17)?

_____

_____

_____

_____

_____

_____

Photographic reproduction of "Monk Reading Book" by Jean-Baptiste-Camille Corot

COMMIT—DAY 5
TRUTH AND BEAUTY

Christ and the Samaritan Woman at the Well,
Byzantine Mosaic, Basilica of San Marco, Venice, Italy

Christ and the Samaritan Woman at the Well / Cameraphoto Arte, Venice / Art Resource, NY

Located among the numerous golden scenes found in St. Mark's Basilica in Venice, Italy, this Byzantine mosaic depicts Jesus' encounter with the Samaritan woman at Jacob's well (see John 4:1–43). Its shimmering golden background highlights the importance of the conversation taking place between Jesus and the woman, which St. Pope John Paul II described, saying, "[Jesus] *discusses the most profound mysteries of God with her. He speaks to her of God's infinite gift of love*" (*Mulieris Dignitatem*, 15, emphasis in original).

Rather than presenting us with a single scene, the mosaic is divided into two parts, providing a pictorial narrative. Recall John 4:1–43. What two events are depicted in the mosaic?

_____

_____

The narrative begins on the left with the encounter and conversation between Jesus and the woman. Two of the disciples stand behind Jesus. While not identified, we can discern St. Peter, with his curly white hair and beard, and St. John, whose gospel recounts this story, with his youthful clean-shaven face. Not wanting to inquire of Jesus, St. John directs his attention to St. Peter, "marvel[ing] that [Jesus] was talking with a woman" (John 4:27).

Jesus' whole attention is directed toward the woman, as he extends his right hand in blessing. The woman had come to the well for water, but her pitcher appears empty, as if it is almost parallel to the ground. Instead of reaching her jar towards the well, she reaches out her opened right hand to receive something more precious than the water for which she came.

At the top of the scene, the Latin inscription "*Dat Potum Sane Fons Vivus Samaritine*" proclaims: "A living fountain gives a drink healthily to the Samaritan." While the Latin "*sane*" could be translated as "discreetly," which also applies as the Apostles were initially away when Jesus first encounters the Samaritan woman, "healthily" gives a sense of the healing and spiritual restoration that happens in the woman's life as a result of her encounter with Jesus.

5th century remains of baptistery at Emmaus-Nicopoli

Most interesting about this scene is its portrayal of the well. Byzantine artistic style seeks to depict the reality of a scene more deeply than a literal photograph could ever picture, by showing the viewer the rich meaning inherent in a scene by employing iconic and allegorical symbols. Here, the well, with its four lobes, takes a cruciform shape and recalls the common shape of an early baptistery. Thus in the mosaic's iconography, the well is given baptismal significance. Behind the well is a tree, a likely reminder that in Baptism we are given access to the Tree of Life, from which Adam and Eve and their descendants were cut off after Original Sin. The living waters welling up to eternal life that Jesus speaks of to the Samaritan woman are received at Baptism with the gift of the Spirit and the indwelling of the Holy Trinity in the soul of each of the baptized. Christians viewing this mosaic were to understand that the gift promised to the Samaritan woman had also been given to each of them.

The scene on the right shows the Samaritan woman a second time, but now she is back in the town speaking to its people. Sin had made her an outcast, having to draw water in the heat of mid-day. But after encountering Jesus at the well and receiving forgiveness and salvation, the Samaritan woman becomes a missionary. "Having received a greater and more important gift than mere water from a well, she leaves her jar behind (cf. John 4:28) and runs back to tell her townspeople that she has met the Christ (cf. John 4:29). Her encounter with Jesus restored meaning and joy to her life, and she felt the desire to share this with others" (Pope Francis, Homily, January 25, 2015). The smaller Latin inscription on the right, "*Venite Videte Hoem Quau Dixit Omia Que Fecit*"—"Come, see the man who said everything I have done"—recalls the woman's words as she returns to the town.

Her words, "Come, see..." are also an invitation for us to encounter Jesus in prayer. And as we more deeply encounter Jesus, as we begin to hear and listen to him in our prayer, we too will know the joy of the Samaritan woman and want to share it with others.

Take a moment to journal your ideas, questions, or insights about this lesson. Write down thoughts you had that may not have been mentioned in the text or the discussion questions. List any personal applications you got from the lessons. What challenged you the most in the teachings? How might you turn what you've learned into specific action?

_____

_____

_____

_____

_____

_____

_____

_____

_____

_____

_____

SESSION 3

LECTIO & MEDITATIO: CLIMBING THE FIRST RUNGS

OPENING PRAYER

How lovely is thy dwelling place,
O Lord of hosts!

My soul longs, yea, faints
for the courts of the Lord;
my heart and flesh sing for joy
to the living God.

Even the sparrow finds a home,
and the swallow a nest for herself,
where she may lay her young,
at thy altars, O Lord of hosts,
my King and my God.

Blessed are those who dwell in thy house,
ever singing thy praise!
Blessed are the men whose strength is in thee,
in whose heart are the highways to Zion.
Amen.

—Psalm 84:1–5

Ladder into sky © Bruce Rolff / shutterstock.com

INTRODUCTION

According to an ancient Chinese proverb, "A journey of a thousand miles begins with a single step." And the ascent to God in prayer begins with reaching out for the first rung of the ladder. The last session outlined Guigo the Carthusian's ladder of *lectio divina* and its four steps: *lectio, meditatio, oratio,* and *contemplatio.* In this session we'll take a closer look at the first two rungs of the ladder, *lectio* and *meditatio,* and provide some opportunities to practice these beginning steps of prayer. At first look, *lectio* and *meditatio* sound pretty simple. But in order to practice these well in prayer, we might just need to unlearn some old habits.

CONNECT

What is your favorite thing to talk about with your closest friend?

What comes to mind when you hear the word "meditation"? Does this word have a positive or negative connotation for you? Why?

DISCUSS

CLIMBING THE FIRST RUNGS
Watch the teaching on video. The following is a brief outline of the topics covered.

I. Guigo's Ladder
  A. A "method" of prayer is just the means
  B. The goal is the encounter with God
  C. "Seek in reading and you will find in meditating; knock in mental prayer and it will be opened to you by contemplation."
    —CCC 2654, quoting Guigo the Carthusian

II. Four Rungs
  A. *Lectio* (Reading): "careful study of the Scriptures, concentrating all one's powers on it"
  B. *Meditatio* (Meditation): "busy application of the mind to seek with one's reason the knowledge of the hidden truth"
    1. Eastern meditation tradition focuses on emptying the mind
    2. Christian meditation is the mind focused on and filling itself with truth
    3. Example of Psalm 1—*lectio* might focus on the pattern of the verbs (walks, stands, sits) and *meditatio* might reflect on how the verb

progression relates to the progression of sin

C. *Oratio* (Prayer)

D. *Contemplatio* (Contemplation)

III. *Lectio*—A Closer Look

    A. Slow down; speed reading is not for *lectio*

    B. Give attention to grammar (verbs, nouns, etc.)

    C. Watch for metaphors

    D. *Lectio* and *meditatio* lead to *oratio* (prayer)

        1. Meditation leads to a conversation with God; prayer flows out of meditation

        2. Ebb and flow, back and forth from *lectio*

IV. Example of Genesis 28—Jacob's Dream

    A. Ladder between heaven and earth; angels ascending/descending upon the ladder

    B. Jacob names the place "house of God," Bethel; ladder becomes image of prayer

    C. John 1:51: "angels...ascending and descending upon the Son of Man"—Jesus is the new ladder, the way by which we reach God

    D. Wrestling as a metaphor for prayer, to persevere in prayer is to not let go of God

DISCUSS

1. What was one thing you heard for the first time or that was an "aha" moment for you?

2. How does *lectio* lead naturally into *meditatio*? How might prayer be especially fruitful with an ebb and flow between *lectio* and *meditatio*?

3. In the video Dr. Gray says that Jacob's wrestling with God is a metaphor for prayer. What does it mean to you to wrestle with God in prayer? Are you comfortable with this image of prayer? Why or why not?

MEMORY VERSE

"Blessed are those who dwell in thy house, ever singing thy praise! Blessed are the men whose strength is in thee, in whose heart are the highways to Zion." **—Psalm 84:4–5**

CLOSING PRAYER

Lord Jesus Christ,
you are the ladder of ascent to the Father in heaven.
Guide us in our prayer,
so that through the attentive reading of *lectio*
and the careful reflection of *meditatio*
we may draw closer to you.
May your Holy Spirit open our hearts
and our minds to receive your words.
In your holy name we pray.
Amen.

Young businessman Praying © Charlotte Purdy / shutterstock.com

FOR FURTHER READING

Tim Gray, "Chapter 3: Lectio" and "Chapter 4: Meditatio" in *Praying Scripture for a Change* **(Ascension Press, 2009)**

Catechism of the Catholic Church **on Sacred Scripture, paragraphs 101–141, and Meditation, paragraphs 2705–2708**

COMMIT—DAY 1
LECTIO: CAREFUL READING

Our modern age emphasizes efficiency. How quickly can a task be accomplished? What is the best way to proceed so that no unnecessary effort is expended? Our rush to accomplish as much as possible, as quickly as possible, makes it difficult to slow down. But that is exactly what we need to do when we practice *lectio*.

Three warning signs to slow down © Chris Pole / shutterstock.com

The goal of *lectio* is not to read as much as possible, as fast as possible, in the time available, but rather to notice as much as possible, trusting that God will direct us to notice what he wants to say to us. Speed-reading is not part of *lectio*. Neither is quantity over quality. Instead, *lectio* requires slow, careful reading—paying attention to the details in the text in order to reap a full harvest from it. Remember, ancient authors didn't include unnecessary words or gratuitous description, since materials were expensive. None of the authors of Sacred Scripture were padding their word count—words were chosen deliberately and carefully, so every word should be read deliberately and carefully to appreciate the full meaning of the passage.

Romantic Couple Walking Through Autumn Woodland © Monkey Business Images / shutterstock.com

So how do we approach a *lectio* text? Careful reading may require reading the passage multiple times—perhaps reading it through at a normal pace to get the big picture, then rereading it at a slower pace, stopping to focus on a particular word or detail as necessary. A good place to begin our focus is simply taking a close look at the grammar of the passage. Paying particular attention to the nouns and verbs used gives the basic information of who is doing what. From there we might give our attention to the adjectives chosen to describe people, places, and things, or to the effect that adverbs give to the words they modify.

Next we can begin to visualize what is going on and imagine ourselves in the passage. We might visualize the surroundings of a particular passage—is this taking place in the city of Jerusalem, or on the Sea of Galilee, or in the hills of Judea? What is the weather—is it hot and sunny, or a cold evening? We might visualize who is present in the passage—is there a crowd, or is it just the disciples, or just one individual and Jesus? And we might put ourselves in the place of one or more individuals in the passage, thinking about what they are thinking and feeling as the passage unfolds. Taking time for this visualization keeps us from a quick, passing perusal of the text, and instead helps us to better understand all that is being communicated. This method of using the imagination to go deeper into Scripture was a favorite tool of St. Ignatius of Loyola.

To illustrate how much difference a single detail can make in understanding a passage, consider the story of God's promise of descendants to Abram in Genesis 15.

> *"And behold, the word of the LORD came to him, 'This man shall not be your heir; your own son shall be your heir.' And he brought him outside and said, 'Look toward heaven, and number the stars, if you are able to number them.' Then he said to him, 'So shall your descendants be.' And he believed the LORD; and he reckoned it to him as righteousness."*   —Genesis 15:4–6

Use the space below to take note of the nouns and verbs in this passage. Read the passage putting yourself into Abram's place. What do you notice based on your careful reading of the passage?

NOUNS	VERBS	ADDITIONAL THINGS NOTICED

The comparison of Abram's "descendants" to the "stars" of heaven gives a beautiful and dramatic illustration of just how numerous Abram's descendants will be, much more so than simply using a word like "multitude" or "nation." The command to "number the stars," and Abram's inability to do so, are a concrete reminder that God alone can fulfill Abram's desire.

Knowing the context of a passage is also an essential component of *lectio*. Imagine going outside your tent in the night and looking toward heaven to count the stars. Now consider the detail revealed a few verses later in Genesis 15:12: "As the sun was going down . . ." God's words in verses 4–6 are spoken in broad daylight.

How does this detail change your visualization and understanding of the passage?

_____

_____

Now try it on your own using the following passage from Psalm 42:1–3:

> *"As a deer longs for flowing streams,*
> *so longs my soul for you, O God.*
> *My soul thirsts for God, for the living God.*
> *When shall I come and behold the face of God?*
> *My tears have been my food day and night,*
> *while men say to me continually, 'Where is your God?'"*

Lectio—Carefully read the passage. What do you note? What nouns and pronouns are used? What verbs and adverbs are used? What comparisons are made?

_____

_____

_____

Whitetail fawn gets a drink © Sean Donohue Photo / shutterstock.com

Try again using the following passage from Luke 9: 23–26.

> *"And he said to all, 'If any man would come after me, let him deny himself and take up his cross daily and follow me. For whoever would save his life will lose it; and whoever loses his life for my sake, he will save it. For what does it profit a man if he gains the whole world and loses or forfeits himself? For whoever is ashamed of me and of my words, of him will the Son of man be ashamed when he comes in his glory and the glory of the Father and of the holy angels.'"*

Lectio—Carefully read the passage. What do you note? What nouns and pronouns are used? What verbs and adverbs are used? What comparisons are made?

_____

_____

_____

How do you express emphasis? If you are writing something for print, you might make the text **bold** or use *italics* in order to draw your reader's attention to an item of particular importance. But what if you are speaking? How do you emphasize an important point so that your audience will take note and remember it? As any educator will tell you, repetition is key.

Many parts of the Bible were passed on as oral tradition before ever being written down. Other parts, although written down, were intended to be read aloud and taught verbally. Even when the Bible was first written down, it was done so by hand, which isn't conducive to bold and italic emphasis. And so throughout Scripture the sacred authors used repetition in order to highlight key ideas and emphasize crucial points. If we read too quickly we can easily skip over this repetition, seeing it as mere redundancy, and miss an important message from the author.

Read the story of the binding of Isaac in Genesis 22:1–14. How many times is the word "son" used in this passage? How many times is "father" or "Abraham" (which means "father of many/multitude") used in the passage?

_____

_____

The departure of Abraham and Isaac / Erich Lessing / Art Resource, NY

This repetition is not an accident; rather it emphasizes the pathos of the story. Abraham is directed to do an unthinkable act, and while Abraham rises early in obedience, it is with a heavy heart that he does so. Isaac is not Abraham's slave or servant but his son, the son whom we are told in the first verses that Abraham loves. We are also reminded that Isaac is Abraham's *only* son, the single heir for whom Abraham has longed his entire life. He is the heir through whom Abraham's multitude of descendants is to come. Each time "son," "father," and "Abraham" are repeated, we are reminded of the great sacrifice Abraham is asked to offer. Abraham will be spared what he dreads with each step up Mount Moriah; but as Jesus, the beloved Son of God the Father, takes each step up Calvary, Abraham's story should come back to us, foreshadowing the great sacrifice that both Jesus and God the Father make for our salvation.

Repetition in the Bible can show itself as a repeated word(s), as above in Genesis 22, or as a repeated phrase, as in Genesis 1, where we hear God repeatedly say, "It is good," after each day of creation, or a repeated structure, as in the Gospel of Matthew, which progresses with five prominent discourses of our Lord. Repetition in the biblical text is never something to be passed over as mere redundancy. Repetition is like a "rumble strip"—it should wake us up so that we don't miss what God is trying to say.

Look up Genesis 37:23–34. How many times is "robe" repeated in these verses? What is this repetition emphasizing?

_____

_____

In addition to repetition, metaphor is another tool that the sacred writers used extensively. Metaphors equate two items, showing the similarities between the two. The biblical authors use metaphorical images to teach and to create a lasting impression in the mind of the reader. The combination of the meaning and the image painted by the words makes them much more memorable than a more abstract statement. For example, take a look at the following verse from Psalm 18:2:

> "The LORD is my rock, and my fortress, and my deliverer, my God, my rock, in whom
> I take refuge, my shield, and the horn of my salvation, my stronghold."

The psalmist could have described God as providing "security" or "defense," but instead he metaphorically equates God with a rock, fortress, deliverer, refuge, horn, shield, and stronghold. Each of these tangible images clearly conveys the strength and protection we find in God. Each of these metaphors is carefully selected and gives the reader much to think about. A rock is an immovable foundation. A fortress, refuge, and stronghold are strong, substantial places of safety where one takes shelter and finds harbor. A shield and horn are armaments used by a deliverer to provide protection from

Jerusalem old city. King David citadel and part of the wall © Oleg Zaslavsky / shutterstock.com

harm and the attacks of one's enemies. The use of these many metaphors gives the reader a multifaceted look at who God is, much like looking at the varied cuts of a diamond each provide an additional reflection of light and increase the diamond's beauty.

Try it on your own using the following passage from Psalm 23:1–3:

> "The LORD is my shepherd, I shall not want;
> he makes me lie down in green pastures.
> He leads me beside still waters; he restores my soul.
> He leads me in paths of righteousness for his name's sake."

Lectio—What metaphor is used?
What does it teach us about God?

_____

_____

_____

_____

_____

Try it on your own using the following passage from Isaiah 64:8:

> "Yet, O LORD, thou art our Father;
> we are the clay, and thou art our potter;
> we are all the work of thy hand."

Lectio—What metaphor is used?
What does it teach us about God?

_____

_____

_____

_____

_____

COMMIT—DAY 3
LECTIO: JACOB WRESTLES WITH GOD

We have described prayer as a dialogue, but sometimes rather than a peaceful conversation, that dialogue can look more like a wrestling match between ourselves and God, especially when we are struggling with a particular issue or grappling with the difficulty of prayer itself. The story of Jacob wrestling with God in Genesis 32 can encourage and guide us in our own wrestling matches with God.

> **LECTIO:** The practice of praying with Scripture, *lectio divina*, begins with an active and close reading of the Scripture passage. Read the verse below and then answer the questions to take a closer look at some of the details of the passage.

"And Jacob was left alone; and a man wrestled with him until the breaking of the day. When the man saw that he did not prevail against Jacob, he touched the hollow of his thigh; and Jacob's thigh was put out of joint as he wrestled with him. Then he said, 'Let me go, for the day is breaking.' But Jacob said, 'I will not let you go, unless you bless me.' And he said to him, 'What is your name?' And he said, 'Jacob.' Then he said, 'Your name shall no more be called Jacob, but Israel, for you have striven with God and with men, and have prevailed.' Then Jacob asked him, 'Tell me, I pray, your name.' But he said, 'Why is it that you ask my name?' And there he blessed him. So Jacob called that place Peniel, saying 'For I have seen God face to face, and yet my life is preserved.'" —Genesis 32:24–30

Who is named in this passage, and who is not? How many times is the word "name" used? How many mentions of each name are there?

_____

_____

Which actions are attributed to Jacob? Which actions are attributed to God?

_____

_____

What does Jacob want here? What does he receive?

_____

_____

> **MEDITATIO:** *Lectio*, a close reading and rereading, is followed by *meditatio*, time to reflect on the Scripture passage and to ponder the reason for particular events, descriptions, details, phrases, and even echoes from other Scripture passages that were noticed during *lectio*. Take some time now to meditate on the above verse.

"The Bible text speaks to us about a long night of seeking God, of the struggle to learn his name and see his face; it is the night of prayer that, with tenacity and perseverance, asks God for a blessing and a new name, a new reality that is the fruit of conversion and forgiveness. For the believer Jacob's night at the ford of the Jabbok thus becomes a reference point for understanding the relationship with God that finds in prayer its greatest expression. Prayer requires trust, nearness, almost a hand-to-hand contact that is symbolic not of a God who is an enemy, an adversary, but a Lord of blessing who always remains mysterious, who seems beyond reach. Therefore the author of the Sacred text uses the symbol of the struggle, which implies a strength of spirit, perseverance, tenacity in obtaining what is desired. And if the object of one's desire is a relationship with God, his blessing and love, then the struggle cannot fail but ends in that self-giving to God, in recognition of one's own weakness, which is overcome only by giving oneself over into God's merciful hands."   —Benedict XVI, General Audience, May 25, 2011

Knowing and addressing someone by his/her name indicates a certain level of relationship, and naming or renaming someone indicates having authority over that person. Why does Jacob ask his opponent's name? Why does God, who certainly already knows Jacob, ask him his name? What is significant about the change in Jacob's name?

_____

_____

What does Jacob's perseverance in his wrestling match teach us about prayer? Why might it be significant that the wrestling takes place at night and lasts all night, while the blessing comes with the dawn?

_____

_____

Where else in Scripture do you see people wrestling with God in prayer? How do these various examples relate to your own experience in prayer?

_____

_____

> **ORATIO, CONTEMPLATIO, RESOLUTIO:** Having read and meditated on today's Scripture passage, take some time to bring your thoughts to God (*oratio*) and engage God in silence (*contemplatio*). Then end your prayer by making a simple concrete resolution (*resolutio*) to respond to God's prompting of your heart in today's prayer.

_____

_____

"The object of opening the mind, as of opening the mouth, is to shut it again on something solid."
—G.K. Chesterton

In *lectio* we carefully study a passage of Scripture in order to hear the Word of God. Our close reading of the text offers us the "who," "what," "when," and "where." As we step onto the next rung of Guigo's ladder, *meditatio*, we apply our minds to thorough reflection on what we have read in God's Word. We seek a deeper understanding of the text—we explore the "why." Reading gives us the raw material; meditation breaks it open to find the treasure inside.

The meditation called for in *lectio divina* is very much an exercise of the intellect. Unlike Eastern traditions of meditation, the goal is not to relax or achieve some different level of consciousness or to empty oneself. Christian meditation is vigorous and active—it seeks to hear and understand God's Word. Rather than emptying, it renews and fills the mind. As St. Paul exhorts us in Philippians 4:8:

*Saint Francis of Assisi praying in front of a crucifix /
© RMN-Grand Palais / Art Resource, NY*

"Finally, brethren, whatever is true, whatever is honorable, whatever is just, whatever is pure, whatever is lovely, whatever is gracious, if there is any excellence, if there is anything worthy of praise, *think* about these things" (emphasis added).

> *"Meditation is above all a quest. The mind seeks to understand the why and how of the Christian life, in order to adhere and respond to what the Lord is asking…. To meditate on what we read helps us to make it our own by confronting it with ourselves."*
> —CCC 2705–2706

In *meditatio* we reflect on the observations made in *lectio:* Why is this person, place, or item described in this way? Why is this word repeated? What is the significance of this detail? etc. A single verse can give us much to meditate upon. Take for example the following verse from the letter to the Hebrews 4:12:

> *"For the word of God is living and active, sharper than any two-edged sword, piercing to the division of soul and spirit, of joints and marrow, and discerning the thoughts and intentions of the heart."*

In our *lectio*, we carefully read and take notice of the words and expressions. We note the nouns (God, Word of God, sword, joints, marrow, thoughts, intentions), verbs (piercing, discerning), adjectives, adverbs, and descriptions (living, active, sharper, two-edged). We note the metaphor of the Word of God as living, active, and a two-edged sword. Now in *meditatio* we dig deeper. Why living "and" active? (Some things can live and be quite passive, but not the Word of God.) Why a "two-edged" sword? (A two-edged sword can do its work in more than one direction.) What does a sharp sword pierce? (What does the Word of God pierce?) Why the image of joints and marrow? (Joint is where two bones meet and move; marrow is the inmost part of the bone.) Why piercing and discerning? (Must discernment go deep?) Why thoughts and intentions, and not actions? (Must discernment of thoughts actions come first so that actions are also good/true?)

Scripture frequently uses the repetition of a simple word or phrase to allude to an earlier narrative. For example, St. John begins his gospel with "In the beginning" (John 1:1). What do these words call to mind? What kind of tone does this set for the rest of St. John's gospel?

_____

_____

St. John doesn't need to come right out and say "The gospel of Jesus Christ is the story of a new creation and the fulfillment of all that was promised in the old" because this allusion to the opening words of Genesis frames the Gospel in precisely those terms. Recognizing these allusions requires reading the Bible as a unified story and developing a familiarity with that story. As you continue to pray with and study Scripture, these connections between various passages will become easier to spot.

Imagination is another important tool for meditation. The *Catechism* says that "meditation engages thought, imagination, emotion, and desire" (CCC 2708). As mentioned earlier, St. Ignatius of Loyola encouraged his followers to make full use of their imagination when praying with Scripture and to place themselves in a passage in order to understand it better. After noting all the relevant details of the verses in *lectio*, we can use this knowledge of the text as a guide for imagining ourselves to be there, observing or even taking part in the action in the various different roles of the story. This method often yields a new appreciation for the passage and reminds us that Scripture is really directed at each of us personally.

Try it on your own using the following passage from Mark 2:1–5:

> *"And when [Jesus] returned to Capernaum after some days, it was reported that he was at home. And many were gathered together, so that there was no longer room for them, not even about the door; and he was preaching the word to them. And they came, bringing to him a paralytic carried by four men. And when they could not get near him because of the crowd, they removed the roof above him; and when they had made an opening, they let down the pallet on which the paralytic lay. And when Jesus saw their faith, he said to the paralytic, 'My son, your sins are forgiven.'"*

Lectio—Carefully read the passage. What do you note?

_____

_____

Meditatio—Reflect on the meaning of what you noted during *lectio*.

_____

_____

COMMIT–DAY 5
TRUTH AND BEAUTY

Christ in the House of Mary and Martha,

Alessandro Allori, c. 1578-1580, Kunsthistorisches Museum, Vienna, Austria

Christ in the House of Mary and Martha / Erich Lessing / Art Resource, NY

Alessandro Allori was a Florentine painter of the late Mannerist period. In his *Christ in the House of Mary and Martha*, Allori brings to life a scene that St. Luke spends only five verses describing in his gospel (see Luke 10:38–42). Instead of enclosing the encounter in a room, Allori places Jesus and the two sisters outside and bathes them in the luminous light of day, which we see reflected in the faces, garments, and landscape that Allori so richly renders.

49

While the gaze of the sisters automatically directs our attention to Jesus, Allori includes several other symbols in his painting that remind us of Christ. What are they?

_____

_____

St. Luke tells us that Mary "sat at the Lord's feet and listened to his teaching" (Luke 10:39). Here is an image for all *lectio*, for as we carefully read God's Word, we too sit at the Lord's feet with Mary. Allori shows us Mary kneeling before Jesus with a heart so drawn to her Lord and listening so intently to his words that she ever so slightly begins to lean closer so as not to miss a word, a syllable, a repetition, or an emphasis in his teaching. To steady herself, she rests her hands on a book, presumably the Scriptures—a reminder to those viewing Allori's work that the word and teaching that Mary hears audibly in her home, the painting's viewers can also hear for themselves in God's Word.

Christ in the House of Mary and Martha / Erich Lessing / Art Resource, NY

Mary's whole attention is focused on Jesus—so much so that she seems unaware of Martha's work to provide the feast that lades down the table behind Jesus. While Martha had been the one who "received [Jesus] into her house," she is soon "distracted with much serving" (Luke 10:38). The water that we see her drawing from the well in the painting's right background, she brings to Jesus in a glass pitcher with three various shaped and filled water glasses. Martha stops short of stepping into or blocking the dialogue between Mary and Jesus, and instead stands with her own attention fixed on Jesus' face.

Other artistic versions of this biblical scene portray Martha decidedly pointing at Mary, such that we can almost hear Martha's accusation recorded in Luke: "Lord, do you not care that my sister has left me to serve alone? Tell her then to help me" (Luke 10:40). Instead of conflict or antagonism between the two sisters, Allori's painting portrays the complementarity between Mary, who represents the contemplative life, and Martha, who represents the active life, both of which are necessary for the disciple of Christ.

Painting after the Reformation, which set faith and works against one another, Allori keeps these two aspects in harmony, with the faces of both Mary and Martha focused on the face of Christ. While balancing both these aspects of the Christian life, Allori does still subtly communicate the Church's emphasis regarding which of these two must come first. Without any rebuke to Martha, Jesus' left hand directs our attention to Mary. Additionally, engraved on the wall behind the scene we read "*Optimam Partem Elegit*"—"She chose the best part." As St. Gregory the Great reminds us: "The two women signify two dimensions of the spiritual life. Martha signifies the active life as she busily labors to honor Christ through her work. Mary exemplifies the contemplative life as she sits attentively to listen and learn from Christ. While both activities are essential to Christian living, the latter is greater than the former. For in heaven the active life terminates, while the contemplative life reaches its perfection" (*Moralia* 2, 6).

St. Paul reminds us that we were "created in Christ Jesus for good works, which God prepared beforehand, that we should walk in them" (see Ephesians 2:10), but we come to know God's will and the works we should walk in by first sitting at the feet of our Lord in prayer, contemplating his Word.

Take a moment to journal your ideas, questions, or insights about this lesson. Write down thoughts you had that may not have been mentioned in the text or the discussion questions. List any personal applications you got from the lessons. What challenged you the most in the teachings? How might you turn what you've learned into specific action?

_____

_____

_____

_____

_____

_____

_____

_____

_____

_____

_____

SESSION 4

ORATIO: CONVERSATION WITH GOD

OPENING PRAYER

The earth is the LORD's and the fullness thereof,
  the world and those who dwell therein;
for he has founded it upon the seas,
  and established it upon the rivers.

Who shall ascend the hill of the LORD?
  And who shall stand in his holy place?
He who has clean hands and a pure heart,
  who does not lift up his soul to what is false,
  and does not swear deceitfully.

He will receive blessing from the LORD,
  and vindication from the God of his salvation.
Such is the generation of those who seek him,
  who seek the face of the God of Jacob.
Amen.

—Psalm 24:1–6

INTRODUCTION

Do you ever wish that prayer could be as easy as just sitting down and having a great conversation with your best friend? Prayer really can be that *simple*. But neither prayer nor any other meaningful conversation is necessarily *easy*. Even among friends, deep conversations take work—we must have a good relationship, we must have a topic of conversation to share, and we must put in the effort to listen and to reflect before we speak.

These are precisely the elements that make for a fruitful conversation in *lectio divina*. Once we have put in the time to read carefully in *lectio* and reflect thoughtfully in *meditatio*, we are ready to converse deeply with God in *oratio*.

Smiling young women drinking coffee
© *Syda Productions / shutterstock.com*

CONNECT

What makes it easy to have a deep, meaningful conversation with a close friend?

Think of a time when you felt distant from a friend and had a hard time talking with that person. What was getting in the way of conversation?

DISCUSS

CONVERSATION WITH GOD
Watch the teaching on video. The following is a brief outline of the topics covered.

I. Review
   A. Samaritan Woman—"If you knew the gift
      of God..." —the gift is the Word of God
   B. First Steps of Guigo's Ladder
      1. *Lectio*—reading; *meditatio*—breaking open
      2. *Oratio*—conversation
         (don't start here, need first steps)

II. *Oratio*—Prayer, Conversation
   A. St. Augustine as a model of prayer
      1. In *Confessions* we overhear
         St. Augustine's prayer with God
      2. St. Augustine recounts an episode from his
         life, then a Scripture passage, which is God
         responding to St. Augustine
      3. St. Teresa of Avila—St. Augustine's
         Confessions teaches her how to pray

B. Barriers to Prayer—*Confessions* Book 9
    1. Psalm 116:16–17—"O LORD…. You have
       loosed my bonds."
    2. Once St. Augustine turns from his anxieties,
       passions, lusts, etc., his mind is free—"I began
       to speak freely to you O Lord, my God"
    3. Two barriers to *oratio*/conversation with God
       a. Skipping *lectio* and *meditatio*
       b. Moral barriers—Not walking in
         God's will leads to disruption in
         relationship/conversation
    4. Obedience breaks down these barriers
C. Psalms as a School of Prayer—CCC 2587
D. Luke 11
    1. "Our" Father—intimate conversation
    2. "Thy will be done"—greatest hindrance to
       prayer is our ego/pride
    3. Our Father placed between almsgiving
       and fasting in Matthew 6
    4. To converse with love, we have to
       learn to love

DISCUSS

1. What was one thing you heard for the first time or that was an "aha" moment for you?

_____

_____

2. What are some examples of moral barriers to prayer (either general or from personal experience)?
What are some specific ways to overcome these particular barriers?

_____

_____

3. What is your experience with praying the psalms? What is your favorite psalm? Why?

_____

_____

MEMORY VERSE

"Lord, teach us to pray."

—Luke 11:1

CLOSING PRAYER

Heavenly Father, you invite us to approach you in trust
and to lay all our needs before you in prayer.
Help us to turn away from anything that is not of you,
that our hearts and our mouths may be opened
to converse freely with you in prayer.
Teach us to love more perfectly so that our prayer
may be a deeper dialogue of love with you.
We ask this in the name of your Son,
our Lord Jesus Christ.
Amen.

Hands clasped in prayer on Holy Bible © Take Photo / shutterstock.com

FOR FURTHER READING

St. Augustine of Hippo, *The Confessions of St. Augustine*

Tim Gray, "Chapter 5: *Oratio*" in *Praying Scripture for a Change* (Ascension Press, 2009)

Catechism of the Catholic Church on the Psalms, paragraphs 2585–2589, and on the Lord's Prayer, paragraphs 2759–2865

COMMIT—DAY 1
ST. AUGUSTINE: MODEL OF PRAYER

The goal of *oratio* is an honest, heartfelt conversation with God over the subject matter discovered in *lectio* and reflected upon in *meditatio*. This is a time to pour out our thoughts in response to what God has said in his Word. We have noted that there is often an ebb and flow in prayer, and this back-and-forth includes *oratio*. Just because we have reached the third rung of the ladder of prayer doesn't mean we stop listening and meditating. As we speak to God in *oratio*, we remain attentive to his gentle promptings to guide the direction of the conversation.

The more time we spend in *lectio divina*, the more we will find ourselves truly praying with Scripture—not only hearing God's Word spoken to us in the Bible but also using the words of Scripture as our own when we talk to God, as well as recognizing God's response to us in additional words of Scripture that may come to mind.

Saint Augustine in his study / Scala / Art Resource, NY

St. Augustine models this way of dialogue in his *Confessions*. St. Augustine not only pours out his questions and struggles to God, but continues to listen in prayer; he incorporates God's response to him into his writing as well. St. Augustine is so steeped in the Word of God that often his own words naturally contain quotes and allusions to Scripture.

Consider the following passage from the opening lines of the *Confessions*:

> *"Grant me, Lord, to know and understand which is first, to call on Thee or to praise Thee? and, again, to know Thee or to call on Thee? for who can call on Thee, not knowing Thee? for he that knoweth Thee not, may call on Thee as other than Thou art. Or, is it rather, that we call on Thee that we may know Thee? but how shall they call on Him in whom they have not believed? or how shall they believe without a preacher? and they that seek the Lord shall praise Him: for they that seek shall find Him, and they that find shall praise Him."*
> —*The Confessions of St. Augustine*, Book I, Chapter 1,
> taken from E. B. Pusey's translation.

What questions does St. Augustine have for God in this passage?

_____

_____

Look up the following verses. What answer does St. Augustine find from God in Scripture?

Psalm 22:26 _____

Jeremiah 29:13_____

Romans 10:14_____

St. Augustine learned to hear God's voice in Scripture—the voice of his Savior, Lord, and friend—and to use the words of Scripture as his own when conversing with God. St. Teresa of Avila described prayer saying, "Prayer is a close sharing between friends" (*The Way of Perfection*). The intimate dialogue we witness in St. Augustine's *Confessions* is a beautiful example of the close sharing of *oratio*, and by the grace of God this deep, conversational prayer is within reach for each of us as well.

Let's take a closer look at how *oratio* works by using one of the passages from last session's COMMIT reflections, a passage from Psalm 42:1–3:

> *"As a deer longs for flowing streams,*
> *so longs my soul for you, O God.*
> *My soul thirsts for God, for the living God.*
> *When shall I come and behold the face of God?*
> *My tears have been my food day and night,*
> *while men say to me continually, 'Where is your God?'"*

To reach the third rung, conversation with God, we begin with *lectio*, observing what parts of the text stand out in our reading. From this we have the material for our mind to focus on during *meditatio*, the second rung. Thus, I may be struck by the repetition of the pronoun "my," inviting me to reflect on the personal relationship God desires with me, with "my soul." The verbs regarding "my soul" in this text are not passive or calm, but alert and achingly active—"longs," "thirsts," each speak about a soul that is restless and searching. These observations and reflections lead us to conversation.

A male fallow deer stag drinking water from a stream © Nicky Rhodes / shutterstock.com

What am I, in my deepest heart, most "longing" for? For what or whom do I search? Like St. Augustine, can I speak to God about my restless heart and honestly tell him about my deepest desires and recognize in them my own search for God? Can I come to terms with the difficult yet hard-to-avoid question at the end, "Where is my God?" In the dialogue with God called *oratio*, it is good to take up the language of the text and to feel free to modify it in your open conversation with God, changing "your" to "my" God—making the text a springboard for your own dialogue with God. Conversation with God leads us to an encounter, and such encounters can end with a deeper sense of consolation, as we "behold the face of God," or a deeper sense of God's absence, as we say, "Where is your God?" Like the patriarch Jacob, our conversation with God is the doorway to encountering the divine, and sometimes we walk away limping, but we never leave the conversation the same. This conversation with God, however, is that for which our heart most longs and thirsts.

Try it on your own using the following passage from John 5:2–9:

"Now there is in Jerusalem by the Sheep Gate a pool, in Hebrew called Bethzatha [Bethesda], which has five porticoes. In these lay a multitude of invalids, blind, lame, paralyzed. One man was there, who had been ill for thirty-eight years. When Jesus saw him and knew that he had been lying there a long time, he said to him, 'Do you want to be healed?' The sick man answered him, 'Sir, I have no man to put me into the pool when the water is troubled, and while I am going another steps down before me.' Jesus said to him, 'Rise, take up your pallet, and walk.' And at once the man was healed, and he took up his pallet and walked."

The Miracle of Bethesda / National Trust Photo Library / Art Resource, NY

Lectio—Carefully read the passage. What do you note?

_____

_____

Meditatio—Reflect on the meaning of what you noted during *lectio.*

_____

_____

Oratio—Journal your conversation with God.

_____

_____

_____

_____

COMMIT—DAY 2
BARRIERS TO CONVERSATION

It's important to remember that *oratio* is the third rung on the ladder of prayer, and not the first. Although we may feel inclined to jump into prayer and try to converse right away, starting with reading and meditation gives us the subject matter for conversation and allows God's Word on that subject to start and shape the dialogue. When we begin at the beginning with *lectio* and *meditatio*, we are much less likely to find ourselves with nothing in particular to say when we speak to God in *oratio*.

Unhappy couple having argument (c) Syda Productions / shutterstock.com

Lack of something to talk about is one barrier to meaningful conversation. Another barrier appears when there is a problem in the relationship. Just as a conversation with a friend or spouse becomes difficult when there is conflict in the relationship, the same happens in our relationship with God when we sin and do not repent. Sin puts a barrier between us and God, the once "close sharing between friends" becomes strained and it is difficult for us to hear God speak.

Scripture describes such a situation:

> *"Behold, the LORD's hand is not shortened, that it cannot save, or his ear dull, that it cannot hear; but your iniquities have made a separation between you and your God, and your sins have hid his face from you so that he does not hear."*
>
> —Isaiah 59:1–2

And then for the next several verses the prophet Isaiah details numerous concrete examples of the sins of God's people that caused this separation: iniquity, lies, unjust law suits, empty pleas, mischief, turning away from following God, etc. Isaiah's words are echoed by the psalmist, "If I had cherished iniquity in my heart, the Lord would not have listened" (Psalm 66:18).

How can we have a close sharing with God in prayer when we let something damage the intimacy of our relationship with him? Whenever we place something else before God, we disrupt the close relationship we seek to nurture in prayer: our sins, our attachment to the things of this world, our insistence on our own will rather than obedience to the will of God, etc. These things not only get in the way of an open conversation in prayer, they often lead us to avoid prayer altogether!

Read Psalm 32. How do we break down the barrier of sin and repair our relationship with God?

_____

_____

St. James encourages us: "Draw near to God and he will draw near to you. Cleanse your hands, you sinners, and purify your hearts" (James 4:8). When we turn to God for reconciliation, we can proclaim like St. Augustine, "Thou hast loosed my bonds." What attachments might be hindering your *oratio*? What steps can you take this week to cultivate a deeper intimacy with God and break down any moral barriers to prayer?

_____

_____

> *"For me, prayer is a surge of the heart; it is a simple look turned toward heaven, it is a cry of recognition and of love, embracing both trial and joy."*
> —St. Therese of Lisieux

Practice *lectio*, *meditatio*, and *oratio* using the following passage from Psalm 139:1–6:

> *"O LORD, you have searched me and known me!*
> *You know when I sit down and when I rise up;*
> *you discern my thoughts from afar.*
> *You search out my path and my lying down,*
> *and are acquainted with all my ways.*
> *Even before a word is on my tongue,*
> *behold, O LORD, you know it altogether.*
> *You beset me behind and before,*
> *and lay your hand upon me.*
> *Such knowledge is too wonderful for me;*
> *it is high, I cannot attain it."*

Lectio—Carefully read the passage. What do you note?

_____

_____

Meditatio—Reflect on the meaning of what you noted during *lectio*.

_____

_____

Oratio—Journal your conversation with God.

_____

_____

The disciples often witnessed Jesus going off alone to pray. After one of these times they asked, "Lord, teach us to pray" (Luke 11:1). Writing on the Lord's Prayer, St. Thomas Aquinas notes: "Prayer interprets our desires, as it were, before God.... Now in the Lord's Prayer not only do we ask for all that we may rightly desire, but also in the order wherein we ought to desire them, so that this prayer not only teaches us to ask, but also directs all our affections" (*Summa Theologica* II-II, Q83, A9). Let's reflect on this most perfect prayer taught to us by Jesus himself.

> **LECTIO:** The practice of praying with Scripture, *lectio divina*, begins with an active and close reading of the Scripture passage. Read the verse below and then answer the questions to take a closer look at some of the details of the passage.

Church Sermon on the Mount - Mount of Beatitudes © kavram / shutterstock.com

"But when you pray, go into your room and shut the door and pray to your Father who is in secret; and your Father who sees in secret will reward you.

And in praying do not heap up empty phrases as the Gentiles do; for they think that they will be heard for their many words. Do not be like them, for your Father knows what you need before you ask him.

Pray then like this:
> *Our Father who art in heaven, Hallowed be thy name.*
> *Thy kingdom come. Thy will be done, On earth as it is in heaven.*
> *Give us this day our daily bread;*
> *And forgive us our debts*
> *As we also have forgiven our debtors;*
> *And lead us not into temptation,*
> *But deliver us from evil.*

For if you forgive men their trespasses, your heavenly Father also will forgive you; but if you do not forgive men their trespasses, neither will your Father forgive your trespasses."

—Matthew 6:6–15

What instructions does Jesus give concerning prayer (place, manner, how we address God, etc.)?

_____

_____

Look for the verbs used in the Our Father. What is the first thing we ask for in this prayer? How do the petitions progress? Is there a pattern?

_____

_____

What is required of us in order for our prayer for forgiveness to be heard and answered?

_____

_____

MEDITATIO: *Lectio*, a close reading and rereading, is followed by *meditatio*, time to reflect on the Scripture passage and to ponder the reason for particular events, descriptions, details, phrases, and even echoes from other Scripture passages that were noticed during *Lectio*. Take some time now to meditate on the verse from page 62.

Our meditation is taken from a section of St. Augustine's *Letter to Proba*, which also appears in the Office of Readings (Tuesday, 29th Week in Ordinary Time) in the Liturgy of the Hours.

> *"We need to use words so that we may remind ourselves to consider carefully what we are asking, not so that we may think we can instruct the Lord or prevail on him.*
>
> *Thus, when we say: 'Hallowed be your name,' we are reminding ourselves to desire that his name, which in fact is always holy, should also be considered holy among men. I mean that it should not be held in contempt. But this is a help for men, not for God.*
>
> *And as for our saying: 'Your kingdom come,' it will surely come whether we will it or not. But we are stirring up our desires for the kingdom so that it can come to us and we can deserve to reign there.*
>
> *When we say: 'Your will be done on earth as it is in heaven,' we are asking him to make us obedient so that his will may be done in us as it is done in heaven by his angels.*
>
> *When we say: 'Give us this day our daily bread,' in saying 'this day' we mean 'in this world.' Here we ask for a sufficiency by specifying the most important part of it; that is, we use the word 'bread' to stand for everything. Or else we are asking for the sacrament of the faithful, which is necessary in this world, not to gain temporal happiness but to gain the happiness that is everlasting.*
>
> *When we say: 'Forgive us our trespasses as we forgive those who trespass against us,' we are reminding ourselves of what we must ask and what we must do in order to be worthy in turn to receive.*

When we say: 'Lead us not into temptation,' we are reminding ourselves to ask that his help may not depart from us; otherwise we could be seduced and consent to some temptation, or despair and yield to it.

When we say: 'Deliver us from evil,' we are reminding ourselves to reflect on the fact that we do not yet enjoy the state of blessedness in which we shall suffer no evil. This is the final petition contained in the Lord's Prayer, and it has a wide application. In this petition the Christian can utter his cries of sorrow, in it he can shed his tears, and through it he can begin, continue and conclude his prayer, whatever the distress in which he finds himself. Yes, it was very appropriate that all these truths should be entrusted to us to remember in these very words."

What is the significance of beginning prayer by addressing God as "Our Father"? What does this teach us about prayer in general?

_____

_____

Which of the petitions of the Lord's Prayer stands out the most to you? Why?

_____

_____

In Matthew's gospel, the Lord's Prayer is framed by instructions concerning almsgiving (Matthew 6:1–4) and fasting (Matthew 6:16–18). What relationship do these two practices have to prayer? Why are they so important?

_____

_____

ORATIO, CONTEMPLATIO, RESOLUTIO: Having read and meditated on today's Scripture passage, take some time to bring your thoughts to God (*oratio*) and engage God in silence (*contemplatio*). Then end your prayer by making a simple concrete resolution (*resolutio*) to respond to God's prompting of your heart in today's prayer.

The Sermon on the Mount / Scala / Art Resource, NY

COMMIT—DAY 4
PSALMS: A SCHOOL OF PRAYER

"Prayed and fulfilled in Christ, the Psalms are an essential and permanent element of the prayer of the Church. They are suitable for men of every condition and time." —CCC 2597

The psalms are not only the prayer book of Israel under the Old Covenant—they also play a central role in the prayer life of the New Covenant. As the *Catechism* states, they are essential to the prayer of the Church, both communal and personal. Every Mass includes a reading (often sung) from the psalms. This Responsorial Psalm invites us to respond in prayer to what we hear in the first reading. The various antiphons and hymns taken from the psalms and used in the Mass also unite us in praying with one voice the prayers that God's people have been offering him for millennia.

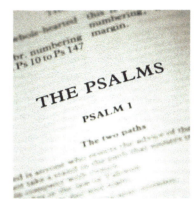

Psalms biblical scriptures © Steve Mann / shutterstock.com

Additionally, in the Liturgy of the Hours the Church systematically prays through the psalms with each four-week cycle. Also known as the Divine Office, these prayers are offered at specific times throughout the day by clergy and religious, and many lay men and women have made participating in at least a portion of this devotion a part of their daily prayer as well.

St. Augustine said that the psalms "serve to mirror ourselves." As Dr. Gray stated in the video, in the psalms we are confronted with ways in which we are like the wicked, and we learn what we must do to be like the righteous. This theme is not only found in the very first psalm, "For the LORD knows the way of the righteous, but the way of the wicked will perish" (Psalm 1:6), but it resonates throughout the entire psalter.

Read Psalm 28. According to this psalm, how do we avoid wickedness? How do we live righteously?

_____

_____

Although they have been prayed in community since they were first written, the psalms are intensely personal prayers. They teach us to pray with complete openness, no matter what we are going through, and they offer examples of prayer arising from a wide range of human emotions and experiences. Mixed in with psalms of adoration, praise, and thanksgiving are psalms of contrition, lament, and even desolation. The psalms teach us not only to pray in every circumstance of our life, but they teach us that even in the midst of trials we can still praise God and his mighty works.

Many of the psalms are written by David and are related to different events of his life—they are personal prayers calling out for God's help in the midst of the very real events of David's life.

Look up the following psalms. What is going on in David's life when he writes each psalm?

Psalm 3 _____

Psalm 51 _____

Psalm 57 _____

While David and others wrote the psalms as personal prayers to God some three thousand years ago, we can pray them as our own in our daily life today.

> *"The marvel with the Psalter is that, barring those prophecies about the Savior and some about the Gentiles, the reader takes all its words upon his lips as though they were his own, and each one sings the Psalms as though they had been written for his special benefit, and takes them and recites them, not as though someone else were speaking or another person's feelings being described, but as himself speaking of himself, offering the words to God as his own heart's utterance, just as though he himself had made them up."*
>
> —St. Athanasius

When we do not know how to "pray as we ought" (Romans 8:26), we should look to the psalms, where the "Word of God becomes man's prayer ... the same Spirit inspires both God's work and man's response" (CCC 2587).

Now try it on your own using the following passage from Psalm 130:1–8:

> *"Out of the depths I cry to you, O Lord! Lord, hear my voice!*
> *Let your ears be attentive to the voice of my supplications!*
> *If you, O Lord, should mark iniquities, Lord, who could stand?*
> *But there is forgiveness with you, that you may be feared.*
> *I wait for the Lord, my soul waits, and in his word I hope;*
> *my soul waits for the Lord more than watchmen for the morning,*
> *more than watchmen for the morning.*
> *O Israel, hope in the Lord! For with the Lord there is steadfast love,*
> *and with him is plenteous redemption.*
> *And he will redeem Israel from all his iniquities."*

Lectio—Carefully read the passage. What do you note?

_____

_____

Meditatio—Reflect on the meaning of what you noted during *lectio*.

_____

_____

Oratio—Journal your conversation with God.

_____

_____

COMMIT—DAY 5
TRUTH AND BEAUTY

King David Playing the Harp, Domenichino, c. 1620, Chateaux de Versailles, France

King David playing the harp / © RMN-Grand Palais / Art Resource, NY

Domenichino (Domenico Zampieri) was an Italian classical Baroque painter, architect, and harp-builder. Bellori, who studied in Domenichino's studio and later wrote his biography, said of him, "He succeeded in delineating the soul, in colouring life, and arousing those emotions in our breasts at which all his works aim." The French king, Louis XIV, so admired Domenichino's *King David Playing the Harp* that he had it installed at his palace at Versailles, initially in the Grand Apartment and then in his personal Interior Apartment, and the painting can be seen today in the palace's Mars Salon.

When we think of David in the Old Testament, often the first things that come to mind are shepherd boy, military warrior, and king of Israel. But we must also add musician and poet.

Look up the following verses. How is David described?

1 Samuel 16:16–23 _____

2 Samuel 6:5 _____

1 Chronicles 16:4–9 _____

Look at the introductory note of the first ten psalms. How many are attributed to David?

_____

Of the total one hundred fifty psalms in the psalter, more than seventy are attributed to David. The New Testament writers also attest to David's authorship of various psalms. When the early Christians rejoice at St. Peter and St. John's release from arrest, they recall the words of David in Psalm 2 (see Acts 4:25). And when the author of the Letter to the Hebrews exhorts the brethren to faith in Christ, he recalls the Spirit speaking through David in Psalm 95 (see Hebrews 3:7–4:7).

King David playing the harp / © RMN-Grand Palais / *Art Resource, NY*

In Domenichino's painting we do not see the young boy looking after his father's sheep, or the victorious military commander, but the crowned king who finally has rest from his enemies. Having set down his sword, he is able to return to the instrument closest to his heart. While Domenichino puts a crown on David's head, he is not seated on the royal throne. Here the emphasis is not on David's kingship, but on the King of kings to whom David sings his praises. David no longer plays on the small lyre or harp that he might have carried with him to the shepherd fields; instead he pulls the strings of a magnificent harp whose resounding melodious notes would have overflowed the room in which he sits and stirred the hearts of those outside the room's open window.

Scripture describes David as "a man after [God's] own heart" (1 Samuel 13:14). Domenichino has turned David's face and eyes heavenward, to the Lord who has been his strength and shield and to whom David has directed all his prayers. Domenichino places two small angels or cherubs on either side of David. The one in front holds an open book, likely the musical score of David's song. The one behind has quill pen and paper and appears to write the words that pour forth from David's heart. These two muses of David's heavenly music express the divine inspiration of David's psalms.

Domenichino, who was also known for his landscapes, uses the view out the window to portray the beauty of God's creation, a beauty of which David's psalms often sang: "The hills gird themselves with joy, the meadows clothe themselves with flocks, the valleys deck themselves with grain, they shout and sing together for joy" (Psalm 65:12–13). Just as all of God's creation sings in praise of the Creator, so too David's psalms call each of us to offer a continual song of praise to God in our words and deeds:

> "Be glad in the LORD, and rejoice, O righteous,
> and shout for joy, all you upright in heart!"
> —Psalm 32:11

> "Let the righteous rejoice in the LORD, and take refuge in him!
> Let all the upright in heart glory!"
> —Psalm 64:10

> "But let the righteous be joyful; let them exult before God;
> let them be jubilant with joy!"
> —Psalm 68:3

Domenichino's painting draws us into David's song of praise, and as we enter into the scene, David's words can become the words of our own joyful heart by which we praise the Lord of our salvation.

Take a moment to journal your ideas, questions, or insights about this lesson. Write down thoughts you had that may not have been mentioned in the text or the discussion questions. List any personal applications you got from the lessons. What challenged you the most in the teachings? How might you turn what you've learned into specific action?

_____

_____

_____

_____

_____

_____

_____

SESSION 5

CONTEMPLATIO: THE GAZE OF LOVE

OPENING PRAYER

The LORD is my light and my salvation;
whom shall I fear?
The LORD is the stronghold of my life;
of whom shall I be afraid?

One thing have I asked of the LORD,
that will I seek after;
that I may dwell in the house of the LORD
all the days of my life,
to behold the beauty of the LORD,
and to inquire in his temple.

For he will hide me in his shelter
in the day of trouble;
he will conceal me under the cover of his tent,
he will set me high upon a rock.

And now my head shall be lifted up
above my enemies round about me;
and I will offer in his tent
sacrifices with shouts of joy;
I will sing and make melody to the LORD.

Hear, O LORD, when I cry aloud,
be gracious to me and answer me!
Thou hast said, "Seek ye my face."
My heart says to thee,
"Thy face, LORD, do I seek."
Amen.

—Psalm 27:1, 4–8

INTRODUCTION

In the previous session we examined how reading and meditating pave the way to conversing with God in *oratio*. Thus far on the ladder of prayer we have made full use of our minds and hearts in our encounter with God, but at the final step all of the efforts of our soul wait upon the Lord to receive his gift of *contemplatio*. Contemplation is most fully something we receive, rather than achieve, but we can prepare ourselves for it by drawing closer to God in love. As St. Gregory the Great said, "The greatness of contemplation can be given to none but those who love."

Holy Sacrament / Renata Sedmakova
shutterstock.com

CONNECT

Describe a time when you were completely caught up in gazing at someone you love or something you thought was beautiful. What did you feel in that moment? Is what you felt easy to describe?

What is something that you really want, but can't work for or achieve on your own? Think of something you can prepare for but have to wait to receive from someone else.

DISCUSS

> **THE GAZE OF LOVE**
> *Watch the teaching on video. The following is a brief outline of the topics covered.*

I. *Contemplatio*—A Gaze of Love
   A. Described using analogies of tasting and seeing; needs to be shown more than explained
   B. Artists teach us how to see the world in a new way, with a gaze of love (Josef Pieper)
   C. "I gazed upon you in your sanctuary, beholding your glory and your strength" (Psalm 63:2)
   D. St. John Vianney recounts a conversation with an old man: "I look at God and he looks at me, and that is enough"; this man only needed to be in the presence of the Beloved

II. Contemplation—The Fruit of Love
   A. Contemplation takes cultivation

B. St. Teresa Avila—experience of contemplation
   is brief initially, but over time the experience is
   elongated with perseverance in prayer
   and the moral life
C. Experience of presence—not about what we
   say or do, action is irrelevant; "Be still and
   know that I am God" (Psalm 46:10)
D. Elijah—God present in a still small voice, not
   in earthquake, fi re, or wind (1 Kings 19:11–12)
E. Presence of the Beloved; diffi cult/rare because
   we lack love
F. *Lectio/meditatio/oratio*—work of obtaining
   water from a well; *contemplatio*—patient
   reception of a gentle rain from heaven

III. Remember Encounters with God
   A. Israel remembers their encounters with God
      (written down in Torah, celebrated
      in annual feasts)
   B. Blaise Pascal—remembers and writes down
      his encounter with God on 11/23/1654
   C. We do this with natural love—pictures of
      wedding days, wedding rings, pictures
      of a favorite trip
   D. Seek the face of God (like Moses at Sinai;
      David in Psalm 27:8)

DISCUSS

1. What was one thing you heard for the first time or that was an "aha" moment for you?

_____

_____

2. What do you think it means to look at God and have him look at you, and for that to be "enough,"
as the man in St. John Vianney's parish described?

_____

_____

3. Why is it so important to remember our encounters with God, both personally (like Pascal) and
communally (like Israel)? How do you do this?

_____

_____

MEMORY VERSE

"My heart says to thee, 'Thy face, LORD, do I seek.'"

—**Psalm 27:8**

CLOSING PRAYER

Lord Jesus Christ,
thank you for the gaze of love
that you desire to give us in contemplation.
Teach us to cultivate a deeper love for you
and for our neighbor,
that we may be ready to receive your gift of contemplation
and return your gaze of love.
May we always seek your face and your presence diligently.
Amen.

Woman hands on bible © 4 Max / shutterstock.com

FOR FURTHER READING

Thomas Dubay, S.M., *Fire Within: St. Teresa of Avila, St. John of the Cross, and the Gospel—on Prayer* (Ignatius Press, 1989)

Tim Gray, "Chapter 6: *Contemplatio*" in *Praying Scripture for a Change* (Ascension Press, 2009)

St. Teresa of Avila, *Way of Perfection* and *Interior Castle*

COMMIT—DAY 1
CONTEMPLATIO: THE GAZE
AND FRUIT OF LOVE

We like to know that our hard work will pay off. There is something reassuring about knowing that if we put forth the effort then we will reap the rewards. However, not everything in life can be obtained simply by hard work—many things are completely out of our control. At times this might make them that much sweeter to receive, but it also makes the waiting difficult.

So it is with prayer. In *lectio divina* we put forth our full efforts of mind and heart in reading, meditating, and conversing with God—prayer requires this hard, consistent work. But the top of the ladder—the final step in our encounter with God—relies more on his action as we patiently await him. *Contemplatio* culminates with the peaceful rest at the end of the arduous climb of *lectio divina*. Having encountered God, we are finally able to simply receive.

The effort of *lectio*, *meditatio*, and *oratio* prepares our hearts to receive and return God's gaze of love in *contemplatio*. It is not unlike the way a farmer works at carefully cultivating his land and tending his crops. After all his hard work, he must still wait patiently for the harvest before he can enjoy the results. The harvest would not come without his hard work, but all the effort in the world cannot force the fruit to ripen any earlier just because it is the farmer's wish.

Autumn harvest fruits and vegetables © Vitaliy Supertramp / shutterstock.com

Contemplation is the fruit of love, and truly something to be savored. This pinnacle of our encounter with God cannot fully be put into words, and so we use images to attempt to describe it—to show, rather than to explain. Guigo the Carthusian describes it as tasting "the joy of everlasting sweetness." It is the moment when our gaze is completely arrested by God and we rest in his love. Or as the psalmist says, it is the moment when we "taste and see that the LORD is good!" (Psalm 34:8).

Because contemplation is an ineffable experience of love, our capacity for contemplation is only as great as our love for God. It is for this reason that contemplation often seems to be a rare and difficult experience—we do not love enough. As we grow in our love for God and the practice of the virtues, we become better able to receive the gift of contemplation and participate in that gaze of love. As St. Paul writes to the Corinthians, "And we all, with unveiled face, beholding the glory of the Lord, are being changed into his likeness from one degree of glory to another; for this comes from the Lord who is the Spirit" (2 Corinthians 3:18). Our job is to "seek the LORD...seek his presence continually!" (1 Chronicles 16:11) in our consistent prayer and holiness of life, so that our hearts become the new wineskin that can hold the new wine of contemplation.

What can you do to increase your love and virtue and make yourself ready for
contemplatio? Where do you feel your efforts stop and God's gift begins?

_____

_____

Spend some time in *lectio divina* today reflecting
on God's love and his invitation to "come away"
in this passage from Song of Solomon 2:10–13.

> *"Arise, my love, my fair one, and come away;*
> *for lo, the winter is past, the rain is over and gone.*
> *The flowers appear on the earth,*
> *the time of singing has come,*
> *and the voice of the turtledove is heard in our land.*
> *The fig tree puts forth its figs,*
> *and the vines are in blossom;*
> *they give forth fragrance.*
> *Arise, my love, my fair one, and come away."*

Turtle doves in a tree © phugonfire / shutterstock.com

Lectio—Carefully read the passage. What do you note?

_____

_____

_____

Meditatio—Reflect on the meaning of what you noted during *lectio*.

_____

_____

_____

Oratio—Journal your conversation with God.

_____

_____

_____

Contemplatio—Take time to simply rest in God's presence.

COMMIT—DAY 2
ADORATION: AN ENCOUNTER
OF THE BELOVED

"The Church and the world have a great need of eucharistic worship. Jesus waits for us in this sacrament of love. Let us be generous with our time in going to meet Him in adoration and in contemplation that is full of faith . . ."
— Pope St. John Paul II (*Dominicae Cenae*, 3)

When is the last time you went to an adoration chapel? Or stopped by a church to visit our Lord in the tabernacle? What was your experience of prayer during that time?

_____

_____

The Savior / Erich Lessing / Art Resource, NY

What better way to train ourselves for *contemplatio's* mystic gaze of love than to literally fix our gaze on our Beloved, physically present to us in the Eucharist. In Adoration we have the opportunity to practice what we long for in *contemplatio*. Although we cannot force the experience of contemplation, even in the adoration chapel, we can practice a proper disposition for receiving the gift.

When we first began our study of *lectio divina*, we examined some of the various distractions and obstacles to prayer—especially our busy and noisy lives. Adoration offers a refuge from the hustle and bustle that surrounds us. The *Catechism* says, "The choice of a favorable place is not a matter of indifference for true prayer" (CCC 2691). The silence and peace of an adoration chapel provides a favorable place.

> *"What matters most is that you develop your personal relationship with God. That relationship is expressed in prayer. God by his very nature speaks, hears, and replies. Indeed, Saint Paul reminds us: we can and should 'pray constantly' (1 Thessalonians 5:17). Far from turning in on ourselves or withdrawing from the ups and downs of life, by praying we turn towards God and through him to each other, including the marginalized and those following ways other than God's path (cf. Spe Salvi, 33).... There is another aspect of prayer which we need to remember: silent contemplation. Saint John, for example, tells us that to embrace God's revelation we must first listen, then respond by proclaiming what we have heard and seen (cf. 1 John 1:2–3; Dei Verbum, 1). Have we perhaps lost something of the art of listening? Do you leave space to hear God's whisper, calling you forth into goodness? Friends, do not be afraid of silence or stillness, listen to God, adore him in the Eucharist. Let his word shape your journey as an unfolding of holiness."*
> — Pope Benedict XVI, April 19, 2008, Address upon Meeting with
> Young People and Seminarians

Before the Blessed Sacrament we have the perfect opportunity to practice God's exhortation recorded in the psalms: "Be still, and know that I am God" (Psalm 46:10).

Even a quick visit to our Lord in the Eucharist has the potential to help us grow in love. Imagine if a husband and wife only showed affection toward each other when they could spend long periods of time together uninterrupted—how quickly that marriage would run into trouble! Instead, a loving couple finds ways to pay attention to each other and offer tokens of their love and affection with great frequency, even if it is a hurried breakfast together before rushing off to work or a quick kiss while trying to get supper on the table. For the one who loves, every glimpse of the beloved is precious, and every opportunity to show love is a chance to grow in love.

> *"It is pleasant to spend time with him, to lie close to his breast like the Beloved Disciple (cf. John 13:25) and to feel the infinite love present in his heart. If in our time Christians must be distinguished above all by the 'art of prayer', how can we not feel a renewed need to spend time in spiritual converse, in silent adoration, in heartfelt love before Christ present in the Most Holy Sacrament?"*
> —Pope St. John Paul II, *Ecclesia de Eucharistia*, 25

Make time this week to visit our Lord in the tabernacle or adoration chapel, and as you join the Beloved Disciple close to Christ's heart, practice the "art of prayer" using the following passage from Psalm 24:3–6.

> *"Who shall ascend the hill of the LORD?*
> *And who shall stand in his holy place?*
> *He who has clean hands and a pure heart,*
> *who does not lift up his soul to what is false,*
> *and does not swear deceitfully.*
> *He will receive blessing from the LORD,*
> *and vindication from the God of his salvation.*
> *Such is the generation of those who seek him,*
> *who seek the face of the God of Jacob."*

Lectio—Carefully read the passage. What do you note?

_____

_____

Meditatio—Reflect on the meaning of what you noted during *lectio*.

_____

_____

Oratio—Journal your conversation with God.

_____

_____

Contemplatio—Take time to simply rest in God's presence.

COMMIT—DAY 3
LECTIO: ELIJAH AND THE STILL SMALL VOICE

The Old Testament is full of accounts of God's dramatic victories over the enemies of his people. One such victory occurs at Mount Carmel in 1 Kings 18, when the prophet Elijah wins a contest against several hundred priests of the false god Baal. Elijah calls out to God in prayer and God answers, sending fire to consume the water-soaked sacrifice and altar. Because of his victory though, the pagan queen Jezebel seeks Elijah's life, and his success is followed by danger and despair. God directs Elijah to journey to Mount Horeb, where God appeared to Moses and gave Israel the Torah. Here on this holy mountain, Elijah encounters God in an unexpected way.

Elijah asleep / Erich Lessing / Art Resource, NY

LECTIO: The practice of praying with Scripture, *lectio divina*, begins with an active and close reading of the Scripture passage. Read the verse below and then answer the questions to take a closer look at some of the details of the passage.

"*[At Horeb, the mount of God, Elijah] came to a cave, and lodged there; and behold, the word of the LORD came to him, and he said to him, 'What are you doing here, Elijah?' He said, 'I have been very jealous for the LORD, the God of hosts; for the people of Israel have forsaken thy covenant, thrown down thy altars, and slain thy prophets with the sword; and I, even I only, am left; and they seek my life, to take it away.' And he said, 'Go forth, and stand upon the mount before the LORD.' And behold, the LORD passed by, and a great and strong wind rent the mountains, and broke in pieces the rocks before the LORD, but the LORD was not in the wind; and after the wind an earthquake, but the LORD was not in the earthquake; and after the earthquake a fire, but the LORD was not in the fire; and after the fire a still small voice. And when Elijah heard it, he wrapped his face in his mantle and went out and stood at the entrance of the cave.*

"*And behold, there came a voice to him, and said, 'What are you doing here, Elijah?' He said, 'I have been very jealous for the LORD, the God of hosts; for the people of Israel have forsaken thy covenant, thrown down thy altars, and slain thy prophets with the sword; and I, even I only, am left; and they seek my life, to take it away.' And the LORD said to him, 'Go, return on your way to the wilderness of Damascus.... Yet I will leave seven thousand in Israel, all the knees that have not bowed to Baal, and every mouth that has not kissed him.'*"

—1 Kings 19:9–15a, 18

What is God's question for Elijah? Look at 1 Kings 19:7–8. Why is this question unexpected?

_____

_____

How is the voice of God's presence described? What adjectives are used? Look up the definitions for these words.

_____

_____

What is the major repetition in this passage? What is framed by the repetition?

_____

_____

> **MEDITATIO:** *Lectio*, a close reading and rereading, is followed by *meditatio*, time to reflect on the Scripture passage and to ponder the reason for particular events, descriptions, details, phrases, and even echoes from other Scripture passages that were noticed during *lectio*. Take some time now to meditate on the verse on page 79.

On Mount Horeb, Elijah experiences the presence of the Lord in the "still small voice." Quiet. Rest. Peace. Stillness. A gaze of love between Elijah and the God he serves. Here is how St. Teresa of Avila described such an encounter with God to her sisters:

> *"In this way His Majesty shows that He is listening to the person who is addressing Him, and that, in His greatness, He is addressing her, by suspending the understanding, putting a stop to all thought, and, as we say, taking the words out of her mouth, so that even if she wishes to speak she cannot do so, or at any rate not without great difficulty. Such a person understands that, without any sound of words, she is being taught by this Divine Master, Who is suspending her faculties, which, if they were to work, would be causing her harm rather than profit. The faculties rejoice without knowing how they rejoice; the soul is enkindled in love without understanding how it loves; it knows that it is rejoicing in the object of its love, yet it does not know how it is rejoicing in it. It is well aware that this is not a joy which can be attained by the understanding; the will embraces it, without understanding how; but, in so far as it can understand anything, it perceives that this is a blessing which could not be gained by the merits of all the trials suffered on earth put together. It is a gift of the Lord of earth and Heaven, Who gives it like the God He is. This, daughters, is perfect contemplation."*
> —*Way of Perfection*, chapter 25

Have you ever felt that the trials of being faithful to God outweigh the benefits? Have you ever shared Elijah's despair? God meets Elijah where he is at and asks, "What are you doing here?" God isn't surprised to see Elijah at Mount Horeb. It's not a question of whether Elijah followed directions correctly—God sent his angel to direct Elijah to this location. It's a question for Elijah's heart. Elijah's joy in following God no matter the consequences has been lost, and instead there is despair. How does God put Elijah back on track?

_____

_____

Look at how God's voice is described in Psalm 29. Elijah might well have expected to find God in the wind, earthquake, or fire. While God chooses to reveal himself in this way at times, like in the lightning and fire atop Mount Sinai at the Exodus (see Exodus 19:16–20), his preference is the indwelling of our heart (see Ezekiel 36:26–27; 1 Corinthians 3:16). Earthquakes and fires get our attention, but God doesn't just want our attention—he desires relationship. And this relationship brings the "love," "rejoicing," "joy," and "blessing" that St. Teresa describes. Once Elijah recognizes God's presence, what does he do?

_____

_____

What does it mean that Elijah is "jealous" for the Lord? How do his jealously and faithfulness open the door to his encounter with God at Mount Horeb? What does the framing of Elijah's encounter with the repetition noted above teach us?

_____

_____

ORATIO, CONTEMPLATIO, RESOLUTIO: Having read and meditated on today's Scripture passage, take some time to bring your thoughts to God (*oratio*) engage God in silence (*contemplatio*). Then end your prayer by making a simple concrete resolution (*resolutio*) to respond to God's prompting of your heart in today's prayer.

_____

_____

_____

COMMIT—DAY 4
REMEMBERING THE ENCOUNTER WITH GOD

What are some ways you remember and celebrate important moments of your life?

_____

_____

Vintage photo stack © Sociologas / shutterstock.com

Memories are important. Whether it is a wedding, a birth, a special outing with a friend, or the life of a loved one who has died, it is natural to commemorate important events. Our desire to preserve our encounters of love and friendship on the natural level points to a supernatural truth: it is right and good to commemorate our encounters with God as well. This remembering is modeled for us throughout the Scriptures. God's people remembered their encounters with him in the Torah, in the teachings and exhortations of leaders throughout salvation history, in the prayers of the psalms, and in celebration through annual feasts.

In writing down Israel's history in Scripture, the sacred authors record encounter after encounter between God and those he has chosen—from Adam and Eve in the garden to Noah on the ark, from God staying Abraham's hand at the sacrifice of his beloved son to Moses leading the people out of Egypt, from David defeating Goliath to God's protection of the three young men in the fiery furnace—salvation history is the story of how God encounters his people. Key moments of this written record were also celebrated in the annual feasts, such as the feast of Passover which remembers the night when God passed over the houses of the Israelites in Egypt and freed them from slavery (see Exodus 12), or the feast of Tabernacles that remembers God's provision as his people lived in tents/booths and wandered in the desert (see Leviticus 23:34–43; Exodus 16).

The psalms incorporate this remembering of the divine encounter into Israel's prayer. Both psalms of lament and psalms of thanksgiving include reminders about what God did for Israel in the past, in order to inspire them, and us, to trust and to praise God today and always. Read Psalm 77. How does calling to mind Israel's past encounters with God shape the psalmist's prayer?

_____

_____

This repeated remembering, in the feasts, prayers, and writings of God's people, formed their hearts and minds—so much that we find Israel's leaders recounting these encounters in order to teach and encourage the people. On the borders of the Promised Land, Moses recounts the last forty years and the many encounters Israel had with God at Sinai and in the wilderness, exhorting them to be faithful to God and his law as they enter this new land (Deuteronomy 1–4). At the dedication of the Temple, Solomon recalls God's work of creation, the exodus, and his promise to David (1 Kings 8). The prophets' continual exhortation is for Israel to remember God's deeds and thus repent of their sin (for example, Isaiah 46:9; Jeremiah 51:50). In exile, Daniel recalls God's deeds and the peoples' transgression and begs God's mercy (Daniel 9). And as the Old Testament comes to a close, when the Jews are facing persecution from their Greek occupiers, the faithful priest Mattathias commissions his sons to fight for the covenant—and he does so by retelling the story of God's encounters with his people (1 Maccabees 2:49–69).

In the New Testament we see this same remembering at work in the early Church. When the deacon Stephen is arrested and brought before the Sanhedrin, he preaches the gospel to them in terms of the history of Israel encountering God in order to explain how Jesus Christ is the final and definitive encounter with God (Acts 7:1–53). When St. John records Jesus' words to the early churches at Ephesus and Sardis, chastising them for forgetting the love they had at first for the Lord, the exhortation, the remedy, that Christ gives begins with "remember": "Remember then from what you have fallen" (Revelation 2:4–5), "Remember then what you received and heard" (Revelation 3:3).

Preaching of Saint Stephen / Scala / Art Resource, NY

We, too, must make a point to remember our encounters with God. We can begin by journaling the words or verses God puts on our heart during our *lectio*, *meditatio*, and *oratio*. This habit will not only allow us to look back at how God has led us over the past weeks and years, but by it we will be ready to also record those most intimate moments we receive from the Lord in the gift of *contemplatio*—no matter how inadequate words might seem to record the experience of that gaze of love. Like the bread and water that sustained Elijah for his forty-day journey to Mount Horeb (1 Kings 19:8), our memory of these moments of prayer can help us bear any future difficulties.

Spend some time in *lectio divina* today, joining the psalmist and his exhortation to "remember the works" of the Lord using a passage from Psalm 105:1–6.

> *"O give thanks to the LORD, call on his name,*
> *make known his deeds among the peoples!*
> *Sing to him, sing praises to him,*
> *tell of all his wonderful works!*
> *Glory in his holy name;*
> *let the hearts of those who seek the LORD rejoice!*
> *Seek the LORD and his strength,*
> *seek his presence continually!*
> *Remember the wonderful works that he has done,*
> *his miracles, and the judgments he uttered,*
> *O offspring of Abraham his servant,*
> *sons of Jacob, his chosen ones!"*

Lectio—Carefully read the passage. What do you note?

_____

_____

Meditatio—Reflect on the meaning of what you noted during *lectio*.

_____

_____

Oratio—Journal your conversation with God.

_____

_____

Contemplatio—Take time to simply rest in God's presence.

COMMIT—DAY 5
TRUTH AND BEAUTY

St. Augustine and His Mother St. Monica, Ary Scheffer, c. 1846, Louvre Museum, Paris

St. Augustine and His Mother St. Monica / © RMN-Grand Palais / Art Resource, NY

The son of German and Dutch parents, Ary Scheffer was a painter of the nineteenth-century French School, whose style tended more classical than the Romantic Movement of his day. He painted *St. Augustine and His Mother St. Monica* toward the end of his career, at a time when he was focusing more on religious subjects.

In his *Confessions*, St. Augustine relates a personal conversation and profound spiritual moment that he shared with his mother, St. Monica, only days before her death. The painting is simply done, with very little besides the muted water and the shadowed back of a chair to distract our attention.

St. Augustine and his mother St. Monica /
© RMN-Grand Palais / Art Resource, NY

St. Monica, clothed in shades of white, appears ready to leave this earthly world and join the white-robed multitude before the throne of God (see Revelation 7:9–14). St. Augustine, a man of thirty-three years who will spend another forty-three years serving God in the world after his mother's death, is clothed in the more earthy hues of a tawny red. The affection between mother and son is seen in the tender way in which St. Monica holds St. Augustine's hand. The faces of these two saints hold our attention as they behold something we cannot yet see. Their captivated gaze intensifies our longing that we too might experience such an intimate encounter with the Lord.

St. Augustine himself, in Book 9, Chapter 10 of his *Confessions (translated by F. J. Sheed)*, best describes this moment that Scheffer captures on his canvas:

"When the day was approaching on which she was to depart this life—a day that You knew though we did not—it came about, as I believe by Your secret arrangement, that she and I stood alone leaning in a window, which looked inwards to the garden within the house where we were staying, at Ostia on the Tiber; for there we were away from everybody, resting for the sea-voyage from the weariness of our long journey by land. There we talked together, she and I alone in deep joy; and forgetting the things that were behind and looking forward to those that were before (Philippians 3:13), we were discussing in the presence of Truth, which You are (John 14:6, 2 Peter 1:12), what the eternal life of the saints could be like, which eye has not seen nor ear heard, nor has it entered into the heart of man (1 Corinthians 2:9). But with the mouth of our heart we panted for the high waters of Your fountain, the fountain of life which is with You: that being sprinkled from that fountain according to our capacity, we might in some sense mediate upon so great a matter.

And our conversation had brought us to this point, that any pleasure whatsoever of the bodily senses, in any brightness whatsoever of corporeal light, seemed to us not worthy of comparison with the pleasure of that eternal Light, not worthy even of mention. Rising as our love flamed upward towards that Selfsame, we passed in review the various levels of bodily things, up to the heavens themselves, whence sun and moon and minds and speaking and marveling at Your works: and so we came to our own souls, and went beyond them to come at last to the region of richness unending (Ezekiel 34:14), where You feed Israel (Psalm 79:2) forever with the food of truth: and there life is that Wisdom by which all things are made (John 1:3), both the things that have been and the things that are yet to be. But this Wisdom itself is not made: it is as it has ever been, and so it shall be forever: indeed "has ever been" and "shall be forever" and "to be going to be" are not eternal. And while we were thus talking of His Wisdom and panting for it, with all the effort of our heart we did for one instant attain to touch it; then sighing..."

Take a moment to journal your ideas, questions, or insights about this lesson. Write down thoughts you had that may not have been mentioned in the text or the discussion questions. List any personal applications you got from the lessons. What challenged you the most in the teachings? How might you turn what you've learned into specific action?

_____

_____

_____

_____

_____

_____

_____

_____

_____

_____

_____

_____

_____

_____

_____

_____

SESSION 6

RESOLUTIO: PUTTING LOVE INTO ACTION

OPENING PRAYER

I will bless the LORD at all times;
his praise shall continually be in my mouth.
My soul makes its boast in the LORD;
let the afflicted hear and be glad.

O magnify the LORD with me,
and let us exalt his name together!
I sought the LORD, and he answered me,
and delivered me from all my fears.

Look to him, and be radiant;
so your faces shall never be ashamed.

This poor man cried, and the LORD heard him,
and saved him out of all his troubles.
The angel of the LORD encamps
around those who fear him, and delivers them.

O taste and see that the LORD is good!
Happy is the man who takes refuge in him!
Amen.

—Psalm 34:1–8

INTRODUCTION

"Faith in action is love, and love in action is service. By transforming that faith into living acts of love, we put ourselves in contact with God Himself, with Jesus our Lord." These wise words from Blessed Teresa of Calcutta point us toward the final step in our study of prayer: *resolutio*. After encountering God in prayer—and especially sharing in his gaze of love in *contemplatio*, as discussed in the last session—our prayer should naturally lead us to a resolution to love God and our neighbor better. Let's take a closer look at how making a resolution to act in love is necessary in order for our prayer to bear fruit in our lives.

CONNECT

Do you think there are any risks or potential dangers associated with prayer? What might they be?

Do you find it easier to keep broad, sweeping resolutions (e.g., "Be a better person") or smaller, specific resolutions (e.g., "Make my bed first thing every morning")? Why?

DISCUSS

PUTTING LOVE INTO ACTION
Watch the teaching on video. The following is a brief outline of the topics covered.

I. The Vineyard of *Lectio Divina*
   A. *Lectio* – Plucking the grapes (words, images, etc.) from the vine
   B. *Meditatio* – Squeezing out the juice (meaning) —if we stop here, we just have grape juice
   C. *Oratio* – Fermentation (conversation bubbles up)
   D. *Contemplatio* – Aging and enjoying of the wine; "O taste and see that the LORD is good!" (Psalm 34:8)
   E. We can't get "instant" wine; so too, we can't expect instant contemplation
   F. Song of Songs uses images of wine and wine-making; love like fine wine, takes cultivation and has depth to it

II. A Fifth Step—*Resolutio*
   A. *Resolutio*—A practical resolution to put our
      prayer into action
   B. "Be doers of the word, and not hearers
      only, deceiving yourselves" (James 1:22)
   C. St. Francis de Sales warns that without
      resolution, we become like Pharisees
   D. Without resolutions, it is easy to imagine
      ourselves holier than we really are

III. Practical Resolutions
   A. Act on things God brings to you during prayer
   B. Make a specific resolution instead of a
      general one; it needs to be small and particular
   C. Resolution doesn't need to "match" meditation
      exactly; rather, we encounter God in prayer
      and our resolution is a way of doing good
      in response to that encounter
   D. "Action ... moves the believer to make his or
      her life a gift to others in charity"
      (Benedict XVI, *Verbum Domini*, 87)
   E. St. Teresa of Avila (*Interior Castle*) on practical
      application: good works are the aim of prayer,
      and prayer strengthens us for service
   F. Prayer is a means to loving and serving God
      better; but the litmus test is how we love
      and serve others

IV. What to Use for Prayer
   A. The Church gives us a plan for our prayer in
      the Liturgy of the Hours
   B. Books of the Bible—in particular, psalms
      and gospels

DISCUSS

1. What was one thing you heard for the first time or that was an "aha" moment for you?

2. Why is it so important to put prayer into action? What do you think would happen to a prayer life that didn't regularly include *resolutio*?

_____

_____

3. What is your favorite reading material to use for prayer? Why?

_____

_____

MEMORY VERSE

"Be doers of the word, and not hearers only, deceiving yourselves."   —James 1:22

CLOSING PRAYER

Heavenly Father,
grant that our encounter with you in prayer
may always lead us to greater love
and more faithful service of you and our neighbor.
May we always seek to grow in virtue
and be transformed by your love.
We ask this in the name of Jesus our Lord.
Amen.

Pouring red wine from bottle into glass with wooden wine casks in background © Africa Studio / shutterstock.com

FOR FURTHER READING

Pope Benedixt XVI, *Deus Caritas Est* **(2005)**

Tim Gray, "Chapter 7: *Operatio***" in** *Praying Scripture for a Change* **(Ascension Press, 2009)**

Origen, *The Song of Songs: Commentary and Homilies*
Available here: **stanselminstitute.org/files/Origen.pdf**

COMMIT—DAY 1
IMPORTANCE OF A RESOLUTION

The inclusion of *resolutio* as a fifth step after Guigo's four rungs on the ladder of prayer is not so much an addition as it is the transition from our conversation in prayer back into our active lives. As St. James instructs us in his letter, we must not only hear the Word of God (and reflect on it, and converse with God about it), but we must put that word into action. If we do not, we risk deceiving ourselves (see James 1:22).

St. Francis de Sales explains this risk of deception in more detail in his instructions on prayer in his *Introduction to the Devout Life*:

> *"Above all things, my daughter, strive when your meditation is ended to retain the thoughts and resolutions you have made as your earnest practice throughout the day. This is the real fruit of meditation, without which it is apt to be unprofitable, if not actually harmful—inasmuch as to dwell upon virtues without practicing them lends to puff us up with unrealities, until we begin to fancy ourselves all that we have meditated upon and resolved to be; which is all very well if our resolutions are earnest and substantial, but on the contrary hollow and dangerous if they are not put in practice. You must then diligently endeavor to carry out your resolutions, and seek for all opportunities, great or small. For instance, if your resolution was to win over those who oppose you by gentleness, seek through the day any occasion of meeting such persons kindly, and if none offers, strive to speak well of them, and pray for them."*

Consider the strong language that St. Francis de Sales uses in this admonition: meditation can be "harmful," "hollow," and "dangerous." Of course, this isn't meant to scare us away from prayer, as if it were so dangerous that we would be better off *not* risking it. Quite the opposite—we cannot afford *not* to pray! But we must be careful not to fall into the trap described above of merely thinking about holiness and virtue without diligently striving to achieve them. Much like watching Olympic athletes, who make various sporting activities look easy, can delude us into thinking we too can easily ski, or swim, or skate as perfectly. It only takes a few minutes after putting on the skis, or skates, or jumping into the pool to realize how much work went into the "easy" performance—so too in the work of the spiritual life. Resolution in prayer is the safeguard that allows our prayer to bear real fruit in our lives.

Saint Francis of Sales / © RMN-Grand Palais Art Resource, NY

Jesus provides an example of how ending prayer with *resolutio* leads to concrete results. When Jesus prays in the Garden of Gethsemane before his trial and crucifixion, he pours out his heart in *oratio*: "My Father, if it be possible, let this chalice pass from me," and, from that conversation with the Father, Jesus resolves to faithfully follow his Father's will: "nevertheless, not as I will, but as you will" (Matthew 26:39). The prayer and resolution made on the rock of Gethsemane strengthen and sustain Jesus to make the sacrifice of his Passion on the rock of Calvary.

What does our Lord's model of prayer in Gethsemane teach us about the importance of *resolutio*?

_____

_____

Christ on the Mount of Olives / Erich Lessing / Art Resource, NY

While Jesus had the advantage of his divine nature to help him follow through on his resolutions, his divine nature didn't lessen the suffering he experienced as a result of his faithfulness to that resolution in Gethsemane. When our weakened human will would turn away from following through and acting on our resolution, it is exactly to Jesus that we should turn "because [Jesus] himself has suffered and been tempted, he is able to help those who are tempted" (Hebrews 2:18).

Spend some time in *lectio divina* today reflecting on St. James' exhortation to put our prayer into action using the following passage from James 1:19–25:

> *"Know this, my beloved brethren. Let every man be quick to hear, slow to speak, slow to anger, for the anger of man does not work the righteousness of God. Therefore put away all filthiness and rank growth of wickedness and receive with meekness the implanted word, which is able to save your souls. But be doers of the word, and not hearers only, deceiving yourselves. For if any one is a hearer of the word and not a doer, he is like a man who observes his natural face in a mirror; for he observes himself and goes away and at once forgets what he was like. But he who looks into the perfect law, the law of liberty, and perseveres, being no hearer that forgets but a doer that acts, he shall be blessed in his doing."*

Lectio—Carefully read the passage. What do you note?

_____

_____

_____

_____

Meditatio—Reflect on the meaning of what you noted during *lectio*.

_____

_____

_____

_____

Oratio—Journal your conversation with God.

_____

_____

_____

_____

Contemplatio—Take time to simply rest in God's presence.

Resolutio—What small thing can you do today to put your prayer into action?

_____

_____

_____

_____

COMMIT–DAY 2
ACTION AS THE FRUIT OF PRAYER

In our study of prayer and our pursuit of a deeper, more intimate conversation with God through *lectio divina*, it could be easy to begin to view prayer as an end in and of itself. But this would be an error. Our goal is not prayer itself—as if once we have accomplished the right kind of prayer experience we are done. Our goal is love. Prayer is a means to that end; therefore, prayer is ordered toward action.

The Visitation / Scala/Ministero per i Beni e le Attività culturali / Art Resource, NY

"We do well also to remember that the process of lectio divina *is not concluded until it arrives at action (*actio*), which moves the believer to make his or her life a gift for others in charity."*

—Pope Benedict XVI (*Verbum Domini*, 87)

Mary models this truth for us at the very beginning of St. Luke's gospel. After her conversation with God, through his messenger the angel Gabriel at the Annunciation, and her "yes" to God's will, Mary immediately goes "with haste" to visit her elderly kinswoman, Elizabeth, and stays for three months serving and helping Elizabeth in the last months of Elizabeth's pregnancy (see Luke 1). Mary shows us that the love of God experienced in prayer should overflow in love and service of others.

If prayer is a means to an end, does that make it more or less important? Why?

_____

_____

Action is a natural and necessary outcome of prayer. With the help of St. Francis de Sales, we have seen how prayer—if it is not followed by action—has the potential to make us puffed up with pride over virtues we have merely meditated on and not yet mastered. It is only when prayer leads to action that it has the power to transform our lives.

Service is both the fruit, and the evidence, of prayer. How can we say that we are truly encountering God, who is Love, in prayer if we then fail to love the people around us? Look up James 2:14–26. How does the relationship between faith and works, as described by St. James, shed light on the relationship between prayer and action?

_____

_____

"This is the end and aim of prayer, my daughters; this is the reason of the spiritual marriage whose children are always good works. Works are the unmistakable sign which shows these favors come from God, as I told you. It will do me little good to be deeply recollected when alone, making acts of the virtues, planning and promising to do wonders in God's service, if afterwards, when occasion offers, I do just the opposite.... This, my sisters, is what I would have us strive for—to offer our petitions and to practice prayer, not for our own enjoyment but to gain strength to serve God."

—St. Teresa of Avila, *Interior Castle*, Seventh Mansion, Chapter 4

Prayer strengthens us for the service of God, and this service takes form not only in our worship of God but also in our love of neighbor. We serve God when we serve those around us.

Spend some time in *lectio divina* today reflecting on how Jesus himself emphasizes the importance of action as the fruit of our prayer using the following passage from Matthew 25:31–40:

"When the Son of man comes in his glory and all the angels with him, then he will sit on his glorious throne. Before him will be gathered all the nations, and he will separate them one from another as a shepherd separates the sheep from the goats, and he will place the sheep at his right hand, but the goats at the left. Then the King will say to those at his right hand, 'Come, O blessed of my Father, inherit the kingdom prepared for you from the foundation of the world; for I was hungry and you gave me food, I was thirsty and you gave me drink, I was a stranger and you welcomed me, I was naked and you clothed me, I was sick and you visited me, I was in prison and you came to me.' Then the righteous will answer him, 'Lord, when did we see you hungry and feed you, or thirsty and give you drink? And when did we see you a stranger and welcome you, or naked and clothe you? And when did we see you sick or in prison and visit you?' And the King will answer them, 'Truly, I say to you, as you did it to one of the least of these my brethren, you did it to me.'"

Lectio—Carefully read the passage. What do you note?

_____

_____

Meditatio—Reflect on the meaning of what you noted during *lectio*.

_____

_____

Oratio—Journal your conversation with God.

_____

_____

Contemplatio—Take time to simply rest in God's presence.

Resolutio—What small thing can you do today to put your prayer into action?

_____

Commit—Day 3
Lectio: Over All
These Put on Love

Every dialogue with God in prayer is a face-to-face encounter with Love. This encounter is meant to transform us more and more into the image of Love. In his Letter to the Colossians, St. Paul gives a fervent exhortation detailing how to live out this transformation.

> **LECTIO:** The practice of praying with Scripture, *lectio divina*, begins with an active and close reading of the Scripture passage. Read the verse below and then answer the questions to take a closer look at some of the details of the passage.

"If then you have been raised with Christ, seek the things that are above, where Christ is, seated at the right hand of God. Set your minds on things that are above, not on things that are on earth. For you have died, and your life is hid with Christ in God. When Christ who is our life appears, then you also will appear with him in glory.

Put to death therefore what is earthly in you: fornication, impurity, passion, evil desire, and covetousness, which is idolatry. On account of these the wrath of God is coming. In these you once walked, when you lived in them. But now put them all away: anger, wrath, malice, slander, and foul talk from your mouth. Do not lie to one another, seeing that you have put off the old nature with his practices and have put on the new nature, which is being renewed in knowledge after the image of its creator. Here there cannot be Greek and Jew, circumcised and uncircumcised, barbarian, Scythian, slave, free man, but Christ is all, and in all.

Put on then, as God's chosen ones, holy and beloved, compassion, kindness, lowliness, meekness, and patience, forbearing one another and, if one has a complaint against another, forgiving each other; as the Lord has forgiven you, so you also must forgive. And above all these put on love, which binds everything together in perfect harmony. And let the peace of Christ rule in your hearts, to which indeed you were called in the one body. And be thankful. Let the word of Christ dwell in you richly, teach and admonish one another in all wisdom, and sing psalms and hymns and spiritual songs with thankfulness in your hearts to God. And whatever you do, in word or deed, do everything in the name of the Lord Jesus, giving thanks to God the Father through him."

—Colossians 3:1–17

What does St. Paul contrast in the first section of this passage (verses 1-5)?

_____

_____

What are we to take off or get rid of ("put to death"), and what are we to "put on"?

_____

_____

In the last section of this passage there is a repetition of the command "let" (verses 15 and 16). What are we to let Christ give us? What are these two gifts supposed to accomplish in us?

_____

_____

> **MEDITATIO:** *Lectio*, a close reading and rereading, is followed by *meditatio*, time to reflect on the Scripture passage and to ponder the reason for particular events, descriptions, details, phrases, and even echoes from other Scripture passages that were noticed during *lectio*. Take some time now to meditate on the verses on page 98.

In another letter, Paul summarizes his above exhortation saying, "Put on the Lord Jesus Christ" (Romans 13:14). The more we unite our prayer and our action, the more our life will be "[hidden] with Christ in God" and we will find we have indeed "put on Christ." Let's reflect with Pope Francis on just how important this unity of prayer and action is:

> *"In our Christian life too, dear brothers and sisters, may prayer and action always be deeply united. A prayer that does not lead you to practical action for your brother—the poor, the sick, those in need of help, a brother in difficulty—is a sterile and incomplete prayer. But, in the same way, when ecclesial service is attentive only to doing, things gain in importance, functions, structures, and we forget the centrality of Christ. When time is not set aside for dialogue with him in prayer, we risk serving ourselves and not God present in our needy brother and sister. St. Benedict sums up the kind of life that indicated for his monks in two words:* ora et labora, *pray and work. It is from contemplation, from a strong friendship with the Lord that the capacity is born in us to live and to bring the love of God, his mercy, his tenderness, to others. And also our work with brothers in need, our charitable works of mercy, lead us to the Lord, because it is in the needy brother and sister that we see the Lord himself."*
>
> —Pope Francis, *Angelus*, St. Peter's Square, July 2013

What is the relationship between the "peace of Christ" (verse 15) and the "word of Christ" (verse 16)? How does this passage encourage us in both contemplative prayer and active love?

_____

_____

What does it mean to "do everything in the name of the Lord Jesus" (verse 17)?

_____

_____

St. Paul gives a very similar exhortation in Ephesians 4:25–5:1, ending with "Therefore be imitators of God, as beloved children." What specific things does St. Paul expect us to do in imitation of God? How does prayer prepare us to be imitators of God?

_____

_____

ORATIO, CONTEMPLATIO, RESOLUTIO: Having read and meditated on today's Scripture passage, take some time to bring your thoughts to God (*oratio*) engage God in silence (*contemplatio*). Then end your prayer by making a simple concrete resolution (*resolutio*) to respond to God's prompting of your heart in today's prayer.

_____

_____

_____

Saint Lucy distributing alms to the poor / Gianni Dagli Orti / The Art Archive at Art Resource, NY

Commit—Day 4
Particular vs. General

"Beloved, if God so loved us, we also ought to love one another." —1 John 4:11

Is there someone in your life that is difficult to love, or a situation where you find it especially challenging to serve others? What causes this difficulty?

_____

_____

We cannot love God if we do not love others. After reminding us that we "ought" to love one another, St. John gets more specific, "For he who does not love his brother whom he has seen, cannot love God whom he has not seen" (1 John 4:20). Our love of God must be lived out in a tangible way in relation to those around us. Sometimes this is easy, but we all experience times when choosing to love and serve someone else in particular ways is difficult or even painful. *Resolutio* is especially important for these difficult situations. We are not going to transform our lives by our own power; we need grace and the gift of God's own charity.

> *"The practice of all the virtues is animated and inspired by charity, which 'binds everything together in perfect harmony'.... Charity upholds and purifies our human ability to love, and raises it to the supernatural perfection of divine love."*
>
> —CCC 1827

It is only through prayer, and putting that prayer into action, that we grow in love and improve in virtue.

Just as we are not going to be able to grow in love without prayer, we are not going to succeed in putting our prayer into action without purposeful resolutions. How many times do we make resolutions, such as "get into shape" or "save money," only to fall off the bandwagon because our resolutions are too big and broad? Such resolutions are nice ideas, but they lack the concrete "action items" needed to obtain the goal.

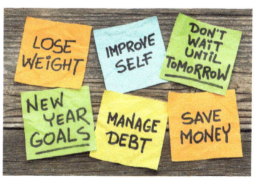

New Year goals or resolutions © marekuliasz / shutterstock.com

The easiest path to success for putting our prayer into action is to make our resolutions small and particular. Instead of the general resolution to "save money," we could make a resolution to pack a lunch for work that day instead of eating out, thus saving the money we would have spent at a restaurant. Instead of a resolution to not "waste time," we could set a time limit on our Internet browsing. St. Francis de Sales gave similar direction in the passage we read on Commit Day 1: "For instance, if your resolution was to win over those who oppose you by gentleness, seek through the day any occasion of meeting such persons kindly, and if none offers, strive to speak well of them, and pray for them." St. Francis de Sales took the general resolution "to win over with gentleness" and refocused it into small, particular actions: "[Meet] such persons kindly" or "speak well of them." Such focused resolutions ready us for action. Although we can still fail or forget, it won't be because we weren't ready with a concrete resolution.

Consider some of the following resolutions that might flow from prayer. How are the particular resolutions more practical than the general ones? Complete the chart by providing examples of specific resolutions to replace the general ones.

General Resolution	Particular Resolution
I will be kind to strangers.	I will smile at and try to make eye contact with each person I see today.
I will be more considerate of others' time.	I will be on time for my appointments today.
I will be more generous with my time.	I will read two bedtime stories to my child instead of rushing through one.
I will not be wasteful.	
I will be more forgiving.	
I will be patient.	
I will take better care of myself.	

Saint ANNE (mother of Virgin Mary) giving to the poor / Alfredo Dagli Orti / The Art Archive at Art Resource, NY

There are several things that might tempt us away from small, focused resolutions in prayer. One temptation is to look at all the areas we need to grow in virtue and love and to feel like reading an extra story to a child or replying to an email promptly isn't really going to make a difference. But we need to remember that just as the ladder of prayer is most easily and successfully climbed one rung at a time, the life of virtue is obtained by adding one small act upon another, habitually.

Another temptation is feeling we need to perfectly relate our *resolutio* to our *lectio* and *meditatio*, and, as a result, we find ourselves unable to arrive at a specific resolution. Sometimes an action will flow very clearly out of our prayer time, but it doesn't need to correspond directly to our topic of reading and meditation. Any resolution to grow in love is a direct response to our encounter with God in prayer, and therefore it is relevant to our *lectio* and *meditatio*, no matter their specific topic.

Spend some time in *lectio divina* today reflecting on St. John's exhortation to love one another using the following passage from 1 John 4:7–12, 20–21:

> *"Beloved, let us love one another; for love is of God, and he who loves is born of God and knows God. He who does not love does not know God; for God is love. In this the love of God was made manifest among us, that God sent his only Son into the world, so that we might live through him. In this is love, not that we loved God but that he loved us and sent his Son to be the expiation for our sins. Beloved, if God so loved us, we also ought to love one another. No man has ever seen God; if we love one another, God abides in us and his love is perfected in us.... If any one says, 'I love God,' and hates his brother, he is a liar; for he who does not love his brother whom he has seen, cannot love God whom he has not seen. And this commandment we have from him, that he who loves God should love his brother also."*

Lectio—Carefully read the passage. What do you note?

_____

_____

Meditatio—Reflect on the meaning of what you noted during *lectio*.

_____

_____

Oratio—Journal your conversation with God.

_____

_____

Contemplatio—Take time to simply rest in God's presence.

Resolutio—What small thing can you do today to put your prayer into action?

_____

_____

COMMIT—DAY 5
TRUTH AND BEAUTY

Clothing the Naked; Works of Mercy—Giving Drink to the Thirsty and Food to the Hungry; and Visiting the Sick; Domenico Ghirlandaio, three of several frescoes in the Oratory of San Martino dei Buonomini, Florence, Italy

Clothing the naked / Scala / Art Resource, NY

Domenico Ghirlandaio was a Florentine Renaissance painter and one of the most accomplished fresco artists of his generation. Ghirlandaio often depicted contemporary figures in the midst of religious narratives, and thus many of his works provide a light into the daily life, dress, and activities of fifteenth-century life. In addition to his extensive work in Florence, he was among those called to Rome to assist with the Sistine Chapel, where he painted the fresco of the *Vocation of the Apostles.*

Ghirlandaio, likely with the help of apprentices in his large and productive workshop (in which Michelangelo was apprenticed and taught early on), produced a series of frescoes in the Oratory of San Martino for the lay confraternity of the Buonomini.

Look up Matthew 25:31–46. What are the works of mercy that Jesus describes?

_____

_____

The confraternity of the Buonomini was founded in 1442 and dedicated to helping the poor, especially needy families who had fallen on hard times. This institution continues its charitable work today. Numerous confraternities existed in medieval society; some focused on devotional aspects (singing of lauds, etc.) and some on charitable works (hospitals, serving the poor, etc.), while others focused on providing devotional and social services for particular artisan groups.

Such lay religious associations were encouraged by the friars and provided a forum for increased attention to moral reform and living a life modeled on the example of Jesus Christ. With this emphasis, those confraternities that focused on charitable works, such as the Buonomini, understood the giving of alms not only as an expression of concern for their neighbor's welfare but also as an expression of piety, a way in which to live a life of charity in imitation of Christ.

Ghirlandaio's *Works of Mercy* frescoes are located in the confraternity's main oratory room, in the ten lunettes formed as the walls meet the arched ceiling. Of the ten total frescoes in the oratory, six present the Buonomini actively engaged in the seven Corporeal Works of Mercy, three of which are represented here in our reflection. The artist's use of perspective allows the activities presented in the frescoes to inhabit their own rooms with arched ceilings to match the oratory room.

Giving Drink to the Thirsty and Food to the Hungry / Scala / Art Resource, NY

In the fresco that incorporates both the works of feeding the hungry and giving drink to the thirsty, a man pours wine into a woman's flask, while behind her, children are handed round loaves of bread. Behind them we can make out a mound of similar loaves of bread ready for distribution— a staple of the Buonomini charitable works was a weekly distribution of bread to those they were assisting. In the fresco showing the work of clothing the naked, a man and woman, possibly husband and wife, are shown in a humble pose, while a young child reaches up for new clothes. Behind them, other men stand behind a *banco* or counter (more typically used for monetary transactions or currency exchange); here they distribute clothes for those without means. In both frescoes we see adults and children, which recalls the Buonomini's emphasis on supporting families with children, especially families in which the head of the household or another member was sick, or families in which a mother was widowed or abandoned by her husband, thus making it difficult for them to provide for themselves. In all the frescoes we see the Buonomini dressed in the traditional cloaks and hoods/hats of fifteenth-century Florentine citizens.

These frescoes not only imaged the works that the Buonomini were doing, they were a constant reminder of Jesus' call upon any who would follow him. In Matthew's gospel, Jesus' ministry begins with his Sermon on the Mount, where Jesus not only directs his disciples to "give to him who begs from you" (Matthew 5:42), but where he also assumes his disciples will do so, thus continuing "*when* you give alms" (Matthew 6:3–4, emphasis added) and where he exhorts them to lay up "treasures in heaven" rather than on earth (Matthew 6:19–20). Jesus ends his teaching ministry on this same note (see Matthew 25:31–46), with the gathering of the nations and the separation of the goats and sheep, with the separation criterion being what one did for those who were hungry, thirsty, naked, homeless, and in prison.

Between these two sermons, Jesus witnessed a life of deep prayer and continual service and care for others, both corporeally (curing the sick, feeding the multitude) and spiritually (forgiving sins, instructing those who followed him, bearing insult, injury, and death). As disciples, the Buonomini heard Jesus' words in the gospels and imitated him, serving those in need around them. As his disciples today, Jesus also calls each of us to a life of intimate conversation and prayer with him, and, by his grace, a life of active service of others.

Visiting the Sick / Scala / Art Resource, NY

Take a moment to journal your ideas, questions, or insights about this lesson. Write down thoughts you had that may not have been mentioned in the text or the discussion questions. List any personal applications you got from the lessons. What challenged you the most in the teachings? How might you turn what you've learned into specific action?

Take a moment to journal your ideas, questions, or insights about this lesson. Write down thoughts you had that may not have been mentioned in the text or the discussion questions. List any personal applications you got from the lessons. What challenged you the most in the teachings? How might you turn what you've learned into specific action?

_____

_____

_____

_____

_____

_____

_____

_____

_____

_____

_____

_____

_____

_____

_____

_____

_____

PRAYER

FINDING INTIMACY WITH GOD

Leader's Resource Guide

LECTIO™

UNVEILING SCRIPTURE AND TRADITION

TIM GRAY

NOTES

TABLE OF CONTENTS

PRAYER:
FINDING INTIMACY WITH GOD

NOTES

WELCOME TO LECTIO

Welcome to the *LECTIO* Study Series. In these sessions of *LECTIO*, your participants will begin to discover the profound importance, meaning, purpose, and beauty of Sacred Scripture and Sacred Tradition, as seen through the eyes of the Church.

LECTIO studies are designed for adult faith formation, to help unveil both Sacred Scripture and Sacred Tradition. The Latin word *lectio* means "reading," and often refers to a careful and prayerful reading of Scripture. These studies cover a wide variety of topics, including individual books or letters of the Bible, the lives and writings of the saints, Church teaching, and topics to help serve the formation of Catholics living out the call of the New Evangelization.

The Leader's Resource Guide, Study Guide, and Session Videos are the three components you will be using for each *LECTIO* session. All three work together to enable a small group to receive the truth of the Catholic Faith and apply it to their everyday lives. We've found that when these resources are used along with your personal witness to the faith, you and your participants can better grow together in knowledge of the Faith and in relationship with Jesus Christ. By leading a *LECTIO* study, you can help participants encounter Jesus Christ and his Church in their own lives, and help them share the faith in the lives of others.

SOME OF THE WAYS TO USE LECTIO

- **Men's & Women's Groups:** For groups of men and women within the parish to grow in the faith through study, discussion, prayer, and service

- **Bible Study Groups:** To explore the profound connections between the Sacred Scriptures and the teachings of the Catholic Church

- **Before/After Mass:** To enrich Catholics' understanding of the Faith and the mysteries of the Liturgy

- **Advent & Lent:** To enhance efforts for ongoing conversion, especially during the seasons of Advent and Lent

- **Catechist Training:** To give those who teach the faith in the parish a more complete and cohesive understanding of the Catholic Faith and to help them express the faith more clearly to those whom they teach

- **Small Christian Communities:** To deepen the growth of parishioners as they participate in a variety of subgroups and apostolates within the parish

- **Families:** As an in-home tool to help parents raise their children to be lifelong disciples of Jesus Christ

- **Individuals:** As a resource for anyone who wants to better understand the Catholic Faith and be equipped to better live it out and explain it to others

LEADING A LECTIO SESSION

The Study Guide takes participants step by step through each session, both the small group gathering and video teaching, as well as five days of follow-up study. The resources are carefully crafted to lead participants through an opening of their hearts and minds to God's Word and the Traditions of the Catholic Church.

The Leader's Resource Guide begins with an introduction of the key points to be covered in each session and includes suggested answers for each of the discussion questions.

WHAT YOU'LL FIND IN EACH LECTIO SESSION:

CONNECT

1. **Opening Prayer:** For this study on prayer, we have chosen specific psalms as a way to grow together in the practice of praying with Scripture. Pope Benedict XVI called the psalms the "prayer book 'par excellence'" and "a school of prayer" for the faithful, and so they are particularly fitting prayers for this study. The Opening Prayer is in the Study Guide, so participants can follow along.

2. **Introduction:** This brief overview of the topic, including the key points for the session, is also located in the Study Guide and should be read aloud following the Opening Prayer. This helps contextualize the topic, show its relevance for daily life, and inspires participants to delve into the particular aspect of the faith that is being presented.

3. **CONNECT Questions:** These first "ice-breaker" questions are provided to get your group talking. As participants watch the video teaching, they will soon find that these questions connect to a theme or topic of the current session.

VIDEO

4. **Video Teaching:** The video segments present teaching that delves into and makes relevant the Sacred Scripture and Sacred Tradition of the Catholic Church. The video teachings for the study on prayer are presented by Dr. Tim Gray, president of the Augustine Institute. The Study Guide includes a brief outline of the key points in the teaching.

DISCUSS

5. **DISCUSS Questions:** Each video segment is followed by questions in the Study Guide to help participants discuss and apply what they have learned to their lives. If you have a large group, consider forming smaller groups for the discussion, with team members facilitating and keeping each small group on track.

   We have included suggested answers for the DISCUSS Questions in this Leader's Resource Guide. Suggested answers can help to get a discussion started, bring greater clarity to the study topic, or answer a difficult question.

6. **Memory Verse:** The participants are encouraged to memorize and reflect on a Scripture verse for every session so as to nurture the faith that has been deepened through your catechetical session.

7. **Closing Prayer:** The Closing Prayer in your Study Guide has been chosen to reflect back to God an appropriate response to his loving action in the session.

8. **For Further Reading:** These additional resources will help participants to nurture their faith throughout the week.

9. **Quotes, Tips, and Definitions:** We have also included throughout the study additional Scripture passages, quotes from saints, and excerpts from other texts and documents such as the *Catechism of the Catholic Church* to help further understanding of a particular topic. You can choose to share this information during the session or direct the participants to it after the session.

COMMIT

The Study Guide includes five COMMIT reflections that will help participants more deeply explore the main topics of each session—and more firmly commit to following Christ in their daily lives. These reflections include more information on Sacred Tradition and Sacred Scripture, as well as topics such as geography, history, and art. These reflections will also include times of prayer, including the practice of Scripture meditation known as *lectio divina*.

AN OVERVIEW OF LECTIO DIVINA

Lectio divina is an ancient practice of enhancing one's prayer life through the power of God's Word. The term itself means "divine reading" of the Sacred Scriptures. It is our hope that by using these simple steps each day as they study Sacred Scripture in LECTIO, participants will develop an effective way to study and pray with God's Word and hear God's voice in their daily lives.

Here is a brief description of each step of *lectio divina* for your reference as you guide participants through the practice:

- **Sacred Reading of the Scriptures (*Lectio*):** The reading and rereading of the Scripture passage, with close attention to words, details, themes, and patterns that speak to you.

- **Meditation (*Meditatio*):** Meditating or reflecting on what you've read, to gain understanding. Allow the Holy Spirit to guide you as you spend time pondering what you have read and striving to understand it in meditation.

- **Prayer (*Oratio*):** A time to bring your meditative thoughts to God in prayer. Talk with God about how the connections and implications of your meditation on the Scripture affect your life and the lives of those around you.

- **Contemplation (*Contemplatio*):** A time of quiet and rest, when you become the receiver and listen to God's voice. Contemplation is a gift from God, not something we achieve on our own—so be patient as you practice this step and strive to be receptive to God's voice speaking into your life.

- **Resolution (*Resolutio*):** A call for resolution and action, inviting you to respond to the things you have read in Scripture and have prayed about and to put them into practice.

To learn more about *lectio divina*, refer to Dr. Tim Gray's book *Praying Scripture for a Change*, available at www.AscensionPress.com.

How To Lead Small Groups

The *LECTIO* Study Series Leader's Resource Guide provides opportunities for small group discussion. Leading a small group discussion does not mean you have to lecture or teach—a successful small group leader facilitates, getting group participants to interact with each other as they make new discoveries. Here are some tips to help you get started as you lead and facilitate your small group:

Environment

- **Make It Friendly:** Set up your meeting space so discussion and conversation happen naturally. Avoid sitting at tables or desks; instead arrange chairs in a circle or meet in a living room environment that encourages casual, friendly conversation. Choose a meeting space that's free of distractions and that offers a fair amount of privacy.

- **Be Tech-Ready:** Make sure you have WiFi or other technology requirements available in your chosen space. Set up and test your audio/video equipment in advance. Queue up videos so they're ready to go to avoid losing valuable discussion time.

- **Consider Refreshments:** Depending on your meeting time, consider offering a light snack so participants won't be distracted by a growling stomach. Even if you don't offer any food items, always have water available for participants.

Logistics

- **Provide Name Tags:** Especially when you first begin meeting, have participants wear name tags so you can easily address them by name and other participants don't have to worry about trying to remember everyone's names.

- **Bring Supplies:** Always have extra pens on hand for people to take notes. Also consider having highlighter pens, paper, and extra materials or Bibles available for participants to use.

- **Be Prompt:** While you can encourage a time to mingle at the beginning of your meeting time, don't let it get out of control so you have to rush through materials and discussion. If people know you're dedicated to starting on time, they'll begin to arrive a bit early to socialize. Likewise, reserve your meeting space for 30 minutes after you're scheduled to end so people can mingle afterward. Be diligent in starting and ending on time.

Before You Meet

- **Prepare:** Look over discussion materials and preview video segments before your meeting time. Go through the questions to make discoveries about how they apply to your own life—this will help you to be more credible as a leader.

- **Pray:** Take time to pray for group members individually and lift up any needs they've expressed during previous meetings. Pray specifically for the Holy Spirit to open the participants' hearts to spiritual growth, renewal, and new discoveries.

- **Evaluate:** As you get to know the needs of individuals and your group's dynamics, evaluate your discussion materials and highlight information or questions that you think would be particularly helpful and insightful for your group.

DURING THE MEETING

- **Set the Tone:** Let group members know from the beginning that your time together is meant to be for discussion and discovery, not lecture. Also remind participants that every question is welcomed and worthy of discussion.

- **Encourage Involvement:** Work to invite all participants to engage in discussion. Don't be afraid of periods of silence, especially during your first few meetings. If one person begins to dominate the discussion time or gets off track, kindly acknowledge the person and invite him or her to explore that topic more after your group time. Ask questions such as "What do the rest of you think?" or "Anyone else?" to encourage several people to respond.

- **Use Open-Ended Questions:** Use questions that invite thought-provoking answers rather than "yes" or "no," "true" or "false," or a one-word, fill-in-the-blank answers. As a leader, your job is to get participants to think about the topic and how the Scriptures and reflections can be relevant and applicable to their daily lives.

- **Affirm Answers:** People are often reluctant to speak up for fear of giving an incorrect answer. Affirm every participant by saying things such as "Great idea," "I hadn't thought of that before," or "That's a great insight." These types of phrases communicate that you value everyone's comments and opinions.

- **Avoid Advice:** Remember, you're acting as a facilitator—not a college professor or counselor. Instead of giving advice or lecturing, when appropriate offer how a Scripture passage or something in the video spoke to you personally, or give an example of how you've been able to apply a specific concept in your own life.

- **Be Flexible and Real:** Sometimes your group time may veer off-track due to something that's going on in our culture or your community (for example, a natural disaster strikes your area or a group member is experiencing a family tragedy). Use relevant topics as a time to model for participants how God is always with us and that we can seek guidance from Scripture, the Church's teachings, and the Holy Spirit in every situation. If you model relevant discussion and transparency, your group participants are more likely to do the same.

- **Transition to Life:** Toward the end of each session, transition discussions toward sharing how participants will apply what has been discussed to their lives in the upcoming week. Close your time together in prayer each time you meet. Invite participants to share requests, either verbally or in writing, so you know how you can pray for them throughout the week.

AFTER THE MEETING

- **Stick Around:** As the leader, make yourself available after your meeting time for questions, concerns, or further discussion on a topic that a participant may have been hesitant about during the scheduled time. If a question arises that has you stumped, admit that you don't have the answer and offer to contact someone who may be able to provide one, such as your parish priest, deacon, or someone else in your diocese.

- **Follow Up:** Making contact with group members during the week will strengthen your relationship. Call or email to see how they're doing at making lessons relevant in their own lives, give a quick encouragement to engage in daily Scripture reading and prayer, or recognize a birthday or anniversary.

SAMPLE 60-MINUTE SESSION

Below is the suggested outline for an hour *LECTIO* session. Use the time allotments as a guideline; the length of time spent on each section will vary from group to group.

	TIME	STEPS	OVERVIEW
CONNECT	2 minutes	Opening Prayer and Introduction	Begin with the Opening Prayer, then go over the Introduction of the session's key points.
	5 minutes	Review	Go over any follow-up questions that participants might have from the previous session's daily COMMIT reflections.
	10 minutes	CONNECT Questions	Present questions to introduce the topic for the current session.
VIDEO	30 minutes	Video	Play the video segments and then facilitate the DISCUSS questions that follow.
DISCUSS	10-15 minutes	DISCUSS Questions	After each video segment, facilitate discussion of the DISCUSS questions in large or small groups.
COMMIT	2 minutes	Summary and Closing Prayer	Summarize the main points from the study, and encourage participants to complete the daily COMMIT reflections.

SAMPLE 90-MINUTE SESSION

Below is the suggested outline for a hour-and-a-half *LECTIO* session. Use the time allotments as a guideline; the length of time spent on each section will vary from group to group.

	TIME	STEPS	OVERVIEW
CONNECT	5 minutes	Opening Prayer and Introduction	Begin with the Opening Prayer, then go over the Introduction of the session's key points.
	10 minutes	Review	Go over any follow-up questions that participants might have from the previous session's daily COMMIT reflections.
	10 minutes	CONNECT Questions	Present questions to introduce the topic for the current session.
VIDEO	30 minutes	Video	Play the video segments and then facilitate the DISCUSS questions that follow.
DISCUSS	20-30 minutes	DISCUSS Questions	After each video segment, facilitate discussion of the DISCUSS questions in large or small groups.
COMMIT	5 minutes	Summary and Closing Prayer	Summarize the main points from the study, and encourage participants to complete the daily COMMIT reflections.

SESSION 1

SESSION OVERVIEW

Read this overview in advance to familiarize yourself with the session.

Prayer is fundamental to the Christian life because we are created by God for an intimate and everlasting relationship with him. But a relationship can't be built or maintained without ongoing conversation with the other person. Despite how basic prayer is to a life of faith, it is not always easy. This session will explore the difficulties we experience in prayer and point us in the right direction of approaching prayer as a conversation.

The *Catechism of the Catholic Church* teaches us that all prayer is a response to God's desire for us— prayer is an encounter that God initiates. When we experience difficulty and dryness in prayer, it's often a result of approaching prayer as a monologue rather than a dialogue. It's important to open our hearts and express our thoughts and feelings in prayer, but if we're only talking and not listening, then prayer cannot be a conversation. We speak to God in prayer, but we must also learn to engage God in silence, especially through the Scriptures. Listening to God speak through the Scriptures is the secret of the saints who mastered the art of prayer.

This session establishes the importance of approaching prayer as a dialogue and emphasizes that Scripture is the normative way in which God speaks to his people. These principles set the foundation for our study.

CONNECT

*Begin this session by leading the **Opening Prayer** and reading aloud the **Introduction**, both found in the Study Guide. Then discuss the following questions.*

What is your earliest memory of praying?

Memories might be from childhood, such as learning a formal prayer like the Our Father, listening to a parent pray out loud at mealtime or bedtime, or being encouraged to talk to God in their own words. Memories might also be from later in life, such as hearing someone else pray and feeling moved, reaching out to God (maybe even before really believing he exists), learning formal prayers, experiencing the Mass for the first time, etc.

If you had to define prayer for someone who had never heard of it, how would you explain it? *Explanations might include defining prayer as an encounter or a conversation with God, thinking of it as talking to a friend. Some might include explanations of formal prayers as both teaching us about God and as articulating our relationship with God. They also might include the rationale behind why we pray— to deepen our relationship with God and to seek and understand his will for our lives.*

 Play the video segment, which will last about 29 minutes. The Study Guide provides participants with a brief outline of the topics covered in the video teaching, along with the following discussion questions.

DISCUSS

After the video segment, discuss the following questions. Familiarize yourself with the comments after each question; these are meant to guide you in the conversation.

AN ENCOUNTER WITH GOD

1. What was one thing you heard for the first time or that was an "aha" moment for you?
Participants might not have realized that finding prayer to be difficult or even a somewhat unpleasant obligation was a common experience. They might not have realized they were treating prayer as a monologue rather than a dialogue. They might not have realized that when they read Scripture, God is speaking to them directly and personally.

2. What obstacles to prayer do you experience? How have you dealt with these in the past? How might approaching prayer as an encounter and a dialogue affect your experience?
There is no end to the obstacles we encounter in prayer: laziness, feeling like it isn't doing any good, simply being busy, setting unrealistic or unsustainable goals and giving up, feeling like we don't know how to pray and not knowing where to start, getting into a rut and not knowing how to get out, etc. Participants may have dealt with these by establishing a set time for prayer, by starting small in the amount of prayer time and in their expectations and increasing these over time, and by reading books or writings on prayer. Approaching prayer as a dialogue can change our focus from "prayer is my job/work" to "prayer is a relationship."

3. Do you feel it is easy or difficult to hear God speaking directly to you in Scripture? Why?
Some participants may have grown up with the understanding that Scripture is meant to be personal—God's love letter to each of us—and so the idea of God speaking to them personally isn't new and may be easier. Others may be used to viewing Scripture as an ancient text and not taking it personally. Some may even feel it is presumptive to read Scripture as God's words directed to them. Some may get hung up on passages that don't seem to apply to them (like laws or genealogies in the Old Testament) and that might get in the way of hearing God in other passages.

*Direct participants to this session's **Memory Verse** in their Study Guides, and read it together. Then lead the **Closing Prayer**. Encourage participants to do the **COMMIT** reflections on their own before you meet again as a group.*

COMMIT

The following are suggested answers to the questions participants will be asked to reflect upon in their daily **COMMIT** *reflections.*

DAY 1 – THE IMPORTANCE OF PRAYER
Participants will explore the importance of prayer as seen in its repeated appearance throughout the Bible.

How do you keep Sunday, the Lord's Day, as a day of prayer? How does this influence the rest of your week?

The first way we keep Sunday as a day of prayer is by participating at Mass—we pray together with the rest of the Church to mark the day as holy and a day of prayer. Other ways may include special family prayer (perhaps a Rosary) or Scripture reading times on Sunday to foster the habit of prayer together. Keeping Sunday a restful day free from unnecessary work or busyness also makes space for prayer and for a spirit of restfulness and quiet that is more conducive to hearing God speak. Hopefully the prayers and readings of the Mass stick with us throughout the week, continuing to bear fruit—and perhaps prompting us to attend daily Mass if possible. Being especially aware of God and the importance of prayer on Sunday can help us improve our habit of prayer throughout the week.

Look up the following psalms: Psalm 73:28 and 105:1–4. Take a moment to recall and praise God for his many works in your own life.

In both these psalms, and many others, the psalmist exhorts us to "tell of all [God's] wonderful works" and to give God thanks. In the monotony of daily life, we can forget the many blessings of God. Remembering these things, small and great, renews in us a spirit of joy and thanksgiving and draws us nearer to God.

What does your life of prayer have in common with prayer as lived throughout Salvation History?

Mass on Sundays and other Holy Days of Obligation corresponds with Israel's liturgical feasts: worshiping God in community and responding together to his invitation to encounter him in prayer. As Catholics we pray the psalms in the Mass and in the Liturgy of the Hours and in many hymns and songs; this unites us with a tradition of prayer that is 3,000 years old. We also face many of the same challenges and difficulties that the Israelites faced in being faithful to God in prayer—and when we fail, as they did, God also calls us back to faithfulness.

DAY 2 – THE PROBLEM OF PRAYER

Participants will look at some of the things that make prayer difficult—especially too much talking on our part and not knowing how to listen.

What are some activities you know to be good and important, but that you simply don't like to do—the ones that always seem to get moved to the bottom of your "to do" list?
Some examples might include: flossing my teeth, going to the dentist, exercising, chores around the house such as vacuuming, folding laundry, or cleaning out the gutters, etc.

What is your greatest struggle with prayer right now?
Struggles might include being so busy that it's difficult to find time for prayer, not knowing how to pray, not feeling like it does any good, or even doubting the efficacy of prayer. When we encounter struggles in prayer, it's important to remember that a difficulty or struggle is not a defeat or failing—in fact, persevering through doubt, difficulty, etc. is virtuous, proving our love and faithfulness.

What are some things you can do to cultivate a habit of exterior and interior silence, and practice the art of patient listening?
Some ideas include setting limits on background noise—both audio and visual. Consider committing to a "media fast"—don't listen to the radio on your drive to work for a few days, or limit the time spent watching movies and videos, etc. Practice giving your full attention to whatever you are doing (no multitasking or daydreaming), and practice active listening in your conversations with friends and family (if you aren't really listening to God, maybe you're not listening 100% to others either). When thoughts or "to do's" interrupt your interior silence, practice setting those aside, maybe by writing them down so that you aren't anxious about forgetting them after your prayer time. Begin by setting small goals for silence and listening in prayer to start and increase slowly over time.

DAY 3 – LECTIO: "I THIRST"

Participants will reflect on Jesus' words from the cross, "I thirst," and how they relate to prayer.

LECTIO

What need or desire does Jesus express in this passage? What does he receive?
Jesus expresses his thirst—both a need for something to satisfy his physical thirst and a passionate desire for each and every one of us. He receives vinegar or sour wine to drink.

What does Jesus give in this passage?
Jesus gives his life, and he gives up his Spirit. He also gives forth water and blood from his side (symbolizing the Sacraments of Baptism and Eucharist, which are received in Christ's Church; the water and blood are also proof that he really died, etc.).

What reason does St. John offer for presenting his testimony in this passage?
St. John says that his reason is "that you also may believe." His whole account of the crucifixion is directed toward inspiring faith—inspiring us to respond to Christ's thirst for us.

MEDITATIO

From the cross Jesus said, "I thirst," and in response he was given vinegar or sour wine—a common drink of the lower classes that, although cheap, was considered refreshing. What does Christ thirst for from you? What can you offer him on a daily basis? Weekly? Over the course of your whole life?

What Christ desires from each of us is our total gift of self to him. We may need to be offering Christ things such as our pride or will so as to conform these more to God's will. Daily we can offer Jesus time in prayer, our love for him lived out in service to others, etc. Weekly offering should include Mass. Long term we can offer Christ ourselves without holding anything back.

The *Catechism* states: "Whether we realize it or not, prayer is the encounter of God's thirst with ours. God thirsts that we may thirst for him. . . . Prayer is . . . a response of love to the thirst of the only Son of God" (CCC 2560–61). Why is it important to understand prayer as a response to God rather than something we initiate? What effect might this view have on your prayer life?

If God initiates prayer, then we need to be listening and responding, not setting our own terms for the encounter. It also takes away some of the burden of prayer being difficult (for example, "It's okay if I'm 'bad' at prayer right now because it doesn't totally depend on me.") But it also lays on us the responsibility to be available to God, to respond to his call to conversation. We might think of prayer as less of something that we have to decide/choose to do, and more of an appointment that has already been set up by God and we just have to show up.

In John 19:28–35, God thirsts for us, but we cannot even respond to him in prayer without his help. From the cross Jesus gives up his Spirit (verse 30), and blood and water flow from his pierced side (verse 34). How do the Holy Spirit and the life of the Church (symbolized by the blood and the water) enable us to respond to God in prayer?

The Holy Spirit teaches us to pray, and the Holy Spirit prays through us (see Romans 8:26). The Church also teaches us to pray by giving us formal prayers to learn and formats for prayer to follow (liturgies). The Church leads us in prayer by drawing us into her liturgies and her communal life of prayer, as well as providing us a community to encourage and help us along in our journey of prayer.

DAY 4 – GOD SPEAKS

Participants will explore the importance of listening to God speak to them personally in Scripture.

Is there a Scripture verse that is particularly meaningful or applicable to your life right now? (It might be something you have memorized, something you heard or read recently, or even something that made an impression but you can't remember the exact verse.)

If participants do not have a passage in mind for this question, here are some passages that may resonate with them:

Psalm 118:24 – "This is the day which the LORD has made; let us rejoice and be glad in it."

Proverbs 3:5–6 – "Trust in the LORD with all your heart, and do not rely on your own insight. In all your ways acknowledge him, and he will make straight your paths."

Jeremiah 29:11 – "For I know the plans I have for you, says the LORD , plans for welfare and not for evil, to give you a future and a hope."

Matthew 6:34 – "Therefore do not be anxious about tomorrow, for tomorrow will be anxious for itself. Let the day's own trouble be sufficient for the day."

1 Corinthians 13:7 – *"Love bears all things, believes all things, hopes all things, endures all things."*

1 Timothy 4:12 – *"Let no one despise your youth, but set the believers an example in speech and conduct, in love, in faith, in purity."*

Consider your current habits for reading Scripture. Do you read from the Bible on a regular basis? Is it for prayer or for study? What are some steps you can take this week to begin praying with Scripture or to increase the time you spend praying with Scripture?

Some participants may already pray with Scripture on a regular basis; others may not have considered the distinction between praying with Scripture and studying Scripture (although both are important and one enhances the other). Concrete steps to take include setting a specific time aside for prayer with Scripture, increasing the existing time, choosing a set place and making it conducive to prayer, possibly getting a Bible without commentaries so as not be distracted when trying to simply pray with the text, picking a specific book of the Bible and reading through it completely rather than skipping around each day, starting the habit of underlining parts of verses in your Bible that touch your heart as your read, etc.

DAY 5 – TRUTH AND BEAUTY

Participants will reflect on Fra Angelico's Annunciation, *c. 1450 in the Convent of San Marco, Florence.*

Look up Luke 1:26–38. In this conversation between God (through his messenger Gabriel) and Mary, who initiates? Is this a monologue, or a dialogue? How does Mary's interaction with Gabriel change over the course of the conversation?

God initiates the conversation by sending Gabriel to Mary and with Gabriel's words, "Hail, full of grace, the Lord is with you!" (Luke 1:28). The conversation is a dialogue as both Gabriel and Mary speak to one another. At first, Mary is perplexed by Gabriel's greeting and considers it in her mind. As Gabriel continues, she dialogues with him, asking him questions about just how God's plan is to come to fruition. As Gabriel continues and she gains understanding, she is able to respond to God's invitation and will for her life. This response comes both in words, "I am the handmaid of the Lord; let it be to me according to your word" (Luke 1:38a), and also in deeds, as she departs to help her elderly kinswoman, Elizabeth (Luke 1:39–40).

NOTES

_____

_____

_____

_____

_____

_____

_____

_____

_____

SESSION 2

SESSION OVERVIEW

Read this overview in advance to familiarize yourself with the session.

In the last session, prayer was described as a conversation that has to go both ways: we not only speak to God in prayer, but we must also listen to God speak to us, especially as we read his Word in Scripture. Much of the difficulty of prayer comes when we make prayer into a monologue and neglect to listen.

St. John's account of Jesus and the Samaritan woman at the well (see John 4:1–43) provides us a model of prayer. This narrative teaches us that God initiates the encounter of prayer and guides us through it. When the Samaritan woman approaches the well, Jesus is already there, and it is he who initiates the conversation. This order recalls the Jewish prayer of the *Shema*—"Hear, O Israel" (Deuteronomy 6:4-5). God speaks, and Israel is to listen. Our first position in prayer is to be the one who listens. If we approach God with humility and listen, then we can ask for what God already knows we need.

As Jesus' conversation with the Samaritan woman continues, Jesus speaks of "living water" (see John 4:10, 14). Here Jesus draws on the words of the prophet Jeremiah, who in telling of Israel's unfaithfulness describes God as the "fountain of living waters" (see Jeremiah 2:13). When we understand this background, we realize that the living water that Jesus promises is his very self.

Dr. Gray closes this session speaking about the twelfth-century monk, Guigo the Carthusian. Guigo describes the order of prayer we call *lectio divina*, the divine reading, as a ladder with four rungs, with each rung carrying us closer to God. The four rungs of the ladder of prayer are: reading, meditation, prayer, and contemplation. This well-worn and established order of prayer helps facilitate our interaction with, and our response to, God. God is ready and waiting for us to meet him in prayer, and Guigo's ladder offers us a clear path from the noise and concerns of our daily lives to communion with God in prayer. With practice we can ascend the ladder with greater ease and more fully reap the fruits of our time with God.

CONNECT

*Begin this session by leading the **Opening Prayer**, and then read or summarize the **Introduction** for your group. Both can be found in the Study Guide.*

*If you have time, review the last session with your group. Can anyone can recite the **Memory Verse**, Song of Solomon 3:2, without assistance? Otherwise, look it up (page 6) and recite it as a group.*

*Also discuss any highlights or questions the group may have had from the last session's **COMMIT** reflections. Then continue.*

Think of a time you felt incredibly thirsty. What quenched your thirst and refreshed you? Describe the experience.

Sample answers include: finding refreshment in a drink of water after a long hike; a cold beer after mowing the lawn on a hot day; etc. There will likely be a common theme of heat and labor causing thirst, followed by a drink that is cool, refreshing, and satisfying. This conversation sets the stage for the story of Jesus asking the Samaritan woman for a drink of water, as well as the contrast between the image of God as "living water" (fresh, flowing water) and the dryness of a broken cistern of our own making (Jeremiah 2:13).

How do you show others that you are listening attentively to them?

Active listening often includes eye contact, responsive motions (nodding the head, facial expressions reflecting what the speaker is talking about, etc.), "listening sounds" such as "mm-hmmm" or other short responses: "Yes, I know what you mean," etc. Answers may include any other aspects of giving someone your full attention, such as putting your phone away, not looking at your watch, asking questions to clarify or continue the conversation on a deeper level. This session focuses on God initiating the conversation of prayer, and so our prayer starts with us listening to God speak—we have to give him our full attention if we want a fruitful conversation.

 Play the video segment, which will last about 29 minutes. The Study Guide provides participants with a brief outline of the topics covered in the video teaching, along with the following discussion questions.

DISCUSS

After the video segment, discuss the following questions. Familiarize yourself with the comments after each question; these are meant to guide you in the conversation.

THE LADDER OF PRAYER

1. What was one thing you heard for the first time or that was an "aha" moment for you?

Some new or particularly striking ideas might include: the comparison between "living water" and a broken cistern, that God is the one who initiates prayer, or the four rungs of the ladder of prayer and why it is important that they proceed in that particular order.

2. How does the account of the Samaritan woman at the well model an encounter with Christ in prayer? How do you relate to this account?

It is a model of prayer because Christ initiates the conversation and the woman responds. There is dialogue. Christ offers living water (the Spirit), and we receive the gift of God in prayer. The conversation opens the eyes of the woman and leads her to a deeper understanding of truth. The encounter changes her. Participants will relate in different ways—some may identify closely with the woman, feeling surprised at God speaking to them, coming to prayer with specific concerns, and leaving with a different understanding of what they really need, etc.

3. Have you ever tried to go straight to the top of the ladder of prayer without making use of the different rungs? Did it work? Do you feel the rungs are evenly spaced (equally easy or difficult to move between each step), or is there one step on the ladder that is particularly hard for you? Why?

*The ladder of prayer will be new to some and may be familiar to others—experience in using the multiple rungs of prayer will vary. Most of us have probably tried, at some point or another, to achieve contemplation without going through the other steps, and without a great deal of practice this usually doesn't work very well. Encourage participants to share which rungs they find easy or difficult—*lectio *and* oratio *may seem to come naturally, but being still and listening in* meditatio *and* contemplatio *may be much harder. Or some may find it difficult to focus during* lectio *or know what to say during* oratio*. A particular rung may be extra difficult because we usually skip it and are out of practice.*

*Direct participants to this session's **Memory Verse** in their Study Guides, and read it together. Then lead the **Closing Prayer**. Encourage participants to do the **COMMIT** reflections on their own before you meet again as a group.*

COMMIT

*Following are suggested answers to the questions participants will be asked to reflect upon in their daily **COMMIT** reflections.*

DAY 1 – HEAR, O ISRAEL
Participants will examine the Shema, *the ancient prayer of Israel, and the importance of listening to God in Israel's theology of prayer.*

God won't let anything get in the way of drawing close to us in prayer. What is getting in your way of listening and responding?
Both internal and external factors get in the way of listening and responding to God in prayer. We might be distracted with our own thoughts; struggling with fear or anger or doubt, which can get in the way of prayer; or letting pride get in the way by relying on ourselves too much when it comes to prayer. We may simply not be giving prayer enough time each day.

DAY 2 – LIVING WATER
Participants will explore the imagery of water as it relates to God in Scripture and study the gift of himself that God offers in prayer.

Look up the following passages: Psalm 65:9; Isaiah 12:3; Isaiah 44:3; Revelation 21:6; Revelation 22:1-2. What do these passages have in common? Why do you think Scripture uses water as an image of God?
In each of these passages, God is described as a life-giving source of water—watering crops (Psalm 65:9); providing salvation as one draws water (Isaiah 12:3); watering the dry ground and pouring out his Spirit (Isaiah 44:3); satisfying thirst, offering forgiveness/eternal life (Revelation 21–22), etc. Water is essential for life, and this fact is particularly well-appreciated in an arid climate such as that of the Holy Land. The image of a life-giving water source communicates God's abundant generosity as well as his sustaining love.

When it comes to prayer, are you actively seeking to receive God's free gift or do you build your own cistern? Do you try to make fruitful prayer happen on your own, or do you let God lead? How can you be more aware of prayer as a gift from God?

We all have experiences of relying on ourselves too much, even in prayer. It may still be a very strong struggle, or it may be something we have largely overcome. Regularly thanking God for the gift of prayer and the gift of himself offered in prayer can be a good reminder that we are receiving his free gift rather than accomplishing something on our own power. Reflecting on and perhaps memorizing one of the Scriptures above about God as living water may also be a useful tool.

DAY 3 – LECTIO: JESUS AND THE SAMARITAN WOMAN
Participants will reflect on the encounter between Jesus and the Samaritan woman at the well.

LECTIO

How many times are "Samaria" and "Samaritans" mentioned in this passage?
Six times (all in the first half of the reading).

How many references are there to thirst or drinking or water in this passage?
Nineteen times (including each reference to the well).

What does the physical setting of this encounter tell you about how Jesus was likely feeling? The Samaritan woman?
The sixth hour means it was noon—heat of the day, no shade. Jesus is weary from his journey, and presumably hungry and thirsty (based on the mention of the disciples going to get food and his request for a drink). The woman is likely hot and tired from her walk to the well. She comes in the heat of the day, alone, so she is isolated from the other women of her village. She may be surprised to find someone else at the well, and perhaps uncomfortable that he speaks to her.

MEDITATIO

Why is the Samaritan woman surprised that Jesus asks her for a drink? What does Jesus' willingness to talk to this woman and St. John's comment on the "necessity" of Jesus passing through Samaria teach us about prayer?
Jews and Samaritans didn't mix, and furthermore Jewish men did not speak to unfamiliar women in public. The Samaritan woman is surprised because "Christ's way of acting, the Gospel of his words and deeds, is a consistent protest against whatever offends the dignity of women" (St. Pope John Paul II, Mulieris Dignitatem, 15) against whatever offends the dignity of his sons and daughters. Jesus' words and actions tell us that God wants to reach out to each of us, despite our sin and brokenness. We can't bridge the gap between ourselves and God on our own, but he can and will.

What is unique about the water that Jesus offers? What do you think it means to never thirst after receiving the living water?
Several things are unique about the water that Jesus offers: it is a gift of God, it is sufficient to satisfy our longing (other things will leave us longing once again), it brings eternal life, etc. One meaning of never thirsting again is that we are created for union with God, and only once we have that relationship will we be satisfied. In the words of St. Augustine: "You have made us for yourself, O Lord, and our hearts are restless until they rest in you."

Jesus tells the Samaritan woman that she would respond differently if she knew who it is that is speaking to her (verse 10). When you pray, are you mindful of "who it is" that is speaking to you? What difference does it make to approach prayer with humility and reverence rather than as something casual and routine?

God is our Father; Jesus is our Lord and our Brother—so there are multiple factors at work in how we approach prayer. It is good to approach God in prayer with both a confidence and a familiarity, but also with an appropriate reverence. Making prayer a priority and remembering to praise and adore God and thank him for his gifts before making requests of him are two ways to practice mindfulness in prayer. Approaching prayer with humility and reverence is crucial because in order to have an intimate conversation and form that close relationship, we have to be honest about who we are in relation to God and be mindful of who God is.

DAY 4 – GUIGO AND THE LADDER OF PRAYER
Participants will explore the four rungs of Guigo's ladder of prayer.

Why must the ladder of prayer begin with Scripture? How might the practice of praying with Scripture help you to fulfill St. Paul's exhortation to "pray constantly" (1 Thessalonians 5:17)?

Prayer begins with Scripture because it is God's Word. It gives us the guidance we need (especially when we are just beginning) to learn how to listen. It gives us something outside of ourselves to focus on and reminds us that we don't accomplish prayer on our own. Praying with Scripture helps us pray constantly by embedding in our hearts and minds a "vocabulary of prayer"—in becoming more familiar with Scripture and how it applies to us specifically, we are more readily able to call it to mind in various situations, which in turn calls us to prayer.

DAY 5 – TRUTH AND BEAUTY
Participants will reflect on Christ and the Samaritan Woman at the Well, *Byzantine Mosaic, Basilica of San Marco, Venice, Italy.*

Rather than presenting us with a single scene, the mosaic is divided into two parts, providing a pictorial narrative. Recall John 4:1-43. What two events are depicted in the mosaic?

The left side of the mosaic depicts Jesus' conversation with the Samaritan woman at the well, including when the Apostles return and unexpectedly find him talking with a woman. The right side of the mosaic recalls how the Samaritan woman goes back to share with her townsfolk the encounter she has had, and to proclaim "the Christ."

NOTES

SESSION 3

Lectio & Meditatio: Climbing the First Rungs

SESSION OVERVIEW

Read this overview in advance to familiarize yourself with the session.

The previous session used the narrative of Jesus and the Samaritan woman at the well to describe and emphasize that God initiates the encounter of prayer. It also briefly outlined Guigo the Carthusian's method of prayer, which he describes using the image of rungs on a ladder: *lectio, meditatio, oratio,* and *contemplatio.* While this method is merely a means to God and not an end in itself, following its steps in order can be a very useful tool—especially when one is still new to *lectio divina* or experiencing difficulty in prayer.

The first rung on the ladder is how we listen to God: *lectio. Lectio* involves a slow, careful reading of the Word of God. Our modern culture with its preference for video, short text messages, and speed-reading, can find this aspect of *lectio* difficult at first. But as we take time and pay closer attention, we will begin to notice how carefully specific words and descriptions are used in God's Word. We will also begin to recognize the different techniques, such as repetition and metaphor, that Scripture uses to get our attention.

The second rung on the ladder is *meditatio,* seeking a deeper understanding in reflection on the passage read in *lectio.* Once careful reading gets us to pay attention to the words God uses, *meditatio* calls us to dig deeper to understand "why." Why is this person, place, or thing described in this way? Why is this word repeated? Why is this description or image used? This reflection will set the stage for a dialogue with God.

These two steps begin our ascent to God in prayer. In reading and meditation we listen attentively to what God says to us in Scripture and focus our minds on understanding his words as fully as possible.

CONNECT

*Begin this session by leading the **Opening Prayer**, and then read or summarize the **Introduction** for your group. Both can be found in the Study Guide.*

*If you have time, review the last session with your group. Can anyone can recite the **Memory Verse** (John 4:10) without assistance? Otherwise, look it up (page 22) and recite it as a group.*

*Also discuss any highlights or questions the group may have had from the last session's **COMMIT** reflections. Then continue.*

What is your favorite thing to talk about with your closest friend?

Topics of conversation with a close friend likely include things that are more personal and meaningful than just shared interests or activities. When talking with a close friend the conversation often becomes a way to share oneself with the other, not just share information. The conversation is motivated by true interest in and care for the other, and a desire to know the other more deeply. This is the type of conversation God wants to have with us in prayer—a deep, personal, sharing of ourselves with God.

What comes to mind when you hear the word "meditation"? Does this word have a positive or negative connotation for you? Why?

Some people may already have experience with the Christian tradition of meditation and so may associate "meditation" with seeking a deeper understanding of truth. However, many people will associate "meditation" with Eastern traditions of meditation that focus more on relaxation, self-awareness, altered consciousness, emptying the mind, etc. There may also be an association with specific postures or activities to aid meditation, such as yoga. For some people the Eastern traditions of meditation will have a negative connotation as they are often closely bound up with religious and philosophic principles not compatible with Christianity.

 Play the video segment, which will last about 30 minutes. The Study Guide provides participants with a brief outline of the topics covered in the video teaching, along with the following discussion questions.

 # DISCUSS

After the video segment, discuss the following questions. Familiarize yourself with the comments after each question; these are meant to guide you in the conversation.

CLIMBING THE FIRST RUNGS

1. What was one thing you heard for the first time or that was an "aha" moment for you?

The Christian tradition of meditation, of filling the mind with truth (as opposed to Eastern traditions which focus on emptying the mind) will likely be new for some participants. The importance of slow reading in lectio, *the examples of different details to observe (such as nouns and verbs, repetition, etc.), and the importance of allusion in* meditatio *may also be new information for some participants.*

2. How does *lectio* lead naturally into *meditatio*? How might prayer be especially fruitful with an ebb and flow between *lectio* and *meditatio*?

*Observing details in the text (*lectio*) leads naturally into reflecting on the significance and deeper meaning of those particular words and the text as a whole (*meditatio*). Because* lectio *requires such slow, careful reading it is natural to stop and meditate at various points in the reading, and then to return to reading until a new point for meditation arises. This ebb and flow allows us to give our full consideration to each point as God draws our attention to it, rather than miss or forget something because we are so focused on reading an entire passage, or on following each step to the letter, that we fail to respond to the Spirit.*

3. In the video Dr. Gray says that Jacob's wrestling with God is a metaphor for prayer. What does it mean to you to wrestle with God in prayer? Are you comfortable with this image of prayer? Why or why not?
Wrestling with God in prayer means persevering in prayer even when it is difficult, continuing to present a petition to God even when he does not seem to be answering, or even arguing with God when we are angry, hurt, confused, etc. We are called to be receptive to God, in order to engage him. Some participants may be comfortable with the image, others may feel it to be too strong or even disrespectful. But wrestling with God in prayer is not about trying to change God's mind/will, but about wrestling with (next to, in accordance with) God in prayer in order to come into line with him and his will for our life.

Direct participants to this session's **Memory Verse** *in their Study Guides, and read it together. Then lead the* **Closing Prayer**. *Encourage participants to do the* **COMMIT** *reflections on their own before you meet again as a group.*

COMMIT

Following are suggested answers to the questions participants will be asked in their daily **COMMIT** *reflections.*

DAY 1 – LECTIO: CAREFUL READING
Participants will learn some tips for reading carefully and paying attention to detail during lectio.

Use the space below to take note of the nouns and verbs in this passage. Read the passage putting yourself in Abram's place. What do you notice based on your careful reading of the passage?
Nouns: word, LORD, man, heir, son, outside, heaven, stars, descendants, righteousness. Verbs: behold, came, shall [not] be, shall be, brought, said, look, number, are able to number, said, believed, reckoned. Additional things noticed: God is the one who is named (LORD); Abram is only referred to by the pronoun "he." God is the one performing the action until the very end, when Abram believed. The words of God's promise and his demonstration to Abram lead Abram to faith. Faith is a response to God.

How does this detail change your visualization and understanding of the passage?
Verse 12 tells us that Abram was told to number the stars while it was daytime, but in the daytime the stars are not visible. It isn't simply a matter of not being able to count high enough to number the stars/his descendants. Abraham can't see the stars in broad daylight, so too he cannot see his descendants—God's point is that Abraham must trust that God will bring his unseen descendants into being, just as the unseen stars will appear when the sun goes down.

Psalm 42:1–3 *Lectio*—Carefully read the passage. What do you note? What nouns and pronouns are used? What verbs and adverbs are used? What comparisons are made?
Nouns: deer, streams, God, face of God, soul, tears, food. Pronouns: "my" is used multiple times. Verbs: longs, thirsts, come and behold, say. Comparisons: my soul is compared to the deer, my longing and thirst compared to the deer's longing for water, my tears are compared to food.

Luke 9:23-26 *Lectio*—Carefully read the passage. What do you note? What nouns and pronouns are used? What verbs and adverbs are used? What comparisons are made?

Nouns: man, cross, life, world, Son, Father, angels, glory. Verbs: come after, follow, deny, take up, save, lose(s), profit, ashamed. Adjectives/Adverbs: not just "man" but "any man"; not just "take up his cross" but take it up "daily"; must lose life "for my sake" in order to save it. Passage also contrasts "profit/gain" and "loss/forfeit."

DAY 2 – LECTIO: REPETITION AND METAPHORS
Participants will learn more tools for lectio by examining the importance of repetition and metaphors.

Read the story of the binding of Isaac in Genesis 22:1-14. How many times is the word "son" used in this passage? How many times is "father" or "Abraham" (which means 'father of many/multitude') used in the passage?

In the story of the binding of Isaac in Genesis 22 we find the word "son" used eleven times in verses 1–14, emphasizing that Isaac was Abraham's long-awaited and much-beloved son. We find the word "father" used two times (on the lips of Isaac, Abraham's son) and the name "Abraham" used fifteen times. The theme of "son" foreshadows Jesus' identity as the only begotten Son of God, sacrificed for our sins. The theme of "father" foreshadows God the loving Father who will offer his only begotten Son.

Look up Genesis 37:23-34. How many times "robe" is repeated in these verses. What is this repetition emphasizing?

The word "robe" is repeated seven times in this passage. In Genesis 37:3 we learn that the "long robe with sleeves" was a gift given to Joseph because his father Israel (Jacob) loved him. For Israel, the robe represents Joseph and the great love of a father for his son. When it reappears torn to pieces, it brings mourning to Israel's heart. For Joseph's brothers, it represents their resentment that their father loves Joseph more than them, and with it they deceive their father (just as Jacob once used the clothes of his brother to deceive his father Isaac—see Genesis 27).

Try it on your own using the passage from Psalm 23:1-3.
Lectio—What metaphor is used? What does it teach us about God?
Psalm 23 uses the metaphor of the LORD as a shepherd, showing that just as a shepherd leads his sheep to good places for their nourishment, so too the LORD leads us in ways of righteousness. As the sheep, I must follow and trust the shepherd.

Try it on your own using the passage from Isaiah 64:8.
Lectio—What metaphor is used? What does it teach us about God?
Isaiah describes God as a potter, and us as clay. In doing so, we come to understand in a deeper way how we must trust God to make each of us into a beautiful work of art. Just as a potter must push and pull on the clay to get it into the right shape, so too as God is working with us. It might not always feel good, but the end result is beautiful.

DAY 3 – LECTIO: JACOB WRESTLES WITH GOD

Participants will reflect on Jacob's wrestling match with God in Genesis 32:24–30 and how this relates to our own prayer.

LECTIO

Who is named in this passage (Genesis 32:24–30), and who is not? How many times is the word "name" used? How many mentions of each name are there?

Jacob is named, God is not. The word "name" is used four times. "Jacob" is used eight times, the "man" is mentioned twice, "Israel" is used once. Just as Jacob receives a name "Israel," Jacob also names the place "Peniel."

Which actions are attributed to Jacob? Which actions are attributed to God?

Jacob is the recipient of several actions (left alone, he is wrestled with, his thigh is put out of joint). Jacob speaks/asks, and names the place. The implied action is that he wrestles and perseveres. God (the "man," God's representative) is portrayed as more active: he wrestles, he sees that he does not prevail, he touches Jacob's thigh and puts it out of joint, he speaks, he changes Jacob's name, and he blesses Jacob.

What does Jacob want here? What does he receive?

Jacob wants a blessing. He receives both a blessing and a new name (and his life, even though he saw God face to face).

MEDITATIO

Knowing and addressing someone by their name indicates a certain level of relationship, and naming or renaming someone indicates having authority over that person. Why does Jacob ask his opponent's name? Why does God, who certainly already knows Jacob, ask him his name? What is significant about the change in Jacob's name?

Jacob doesn't immediately recognize that he is wrestling with God, and so he asks his apparent opponent his name. Jacob is returning to "his country and his kindred" (see Genesis 32:9). When he left his country, he was fleeing for his life because he had hidden his identity and stolen the blessing from his brother Esau. Now as Jacob is about to return home, God asks Jacob, "What is your name?" to give Jacob the chance to be truthful in asking for a blessing. Jacob's name change, from Jacob, which means "supplanter" or "deceiver," to Israel, which means "he who prevails with God," demonstrates the change in Jacob and reflects the change in his relationship with God. As we wrestle with God in our own prayer, God will also ask us questions that will likely reveal our sin so that we can receive his forgiveness, and he will also change us, making us more and more in his own likeness.

What does Jacob's perseverance in his wrestling match teach us about prayer? Why might it be significant that the wrestling takes place at night and lasts all night, while the blessing comes with the dawn?

We should never give up in prayer—never give up due to difficulties, never give up seeking God and asking for his blessing. It also teaches us that sometimes getting an answer in prayer might take longer than we want or expect, but we should stick with it no matter how long it takes. Wrestling in prayer may feel dark and hopeless—like night—but blessing, clarity, and understanding will follow like the dawn. "Weeping may tarry for the night, but joy comes with the morning" (Psalm 30:5).

Where else in Scripture do you see people wrestling with God in prayer? How do these various examples relate to your own experience in prayer?

We see this especially in the psalms, for example when the psalmist is crying out to God to help him in his distress (see for example, Psalm 38, 42, or 88). We see this when St. Paul several times requests that the "thorn in his flesh" be removed, but Christ says, "my grace is sufficient" (see 2 Corinthians 12:7-9). We also see this in Jesus' prayer in the Garden of Gethsemane, where Jesus asks that this cup be taken from him. Seeing Jesus' prayer in this light may make some people more comfortable with the idea of wrestling with God in prayer. It's not about trying to change God's mind/will, but about wrestling with (next to, in accordance with) God in prayer in order to come into line with him and his will for our lives.

DAY 4 – MEDITATIO: STEPPING UP FROM LECTIO
Participants will reflect on meditatio, *Christian meditation.*

Scripture frequently uses the repetition of a simple word or phrase to allude to an earlier narrative. For example, St. John begins his gospel with "In the beginning" (John 1:1). What do these words call to mind? What kind of tone does this set for the rest of St. John's gospel?

These words call to mind the opening words of the Book of Genesis, which also begins, "In the beginning." Genesis' first chapters speak of the first creation of the world. The prophets foretold that God would bring about a new creation (see Isaiah 65:17, for example). By recalling Genesis' opening words at the beginning of his gospel, St. John alludes to the "new creation" that is about to happen in Jesus Christ.

Try it on your own using the passage from Mark 2:1-5.
Lectio—Carefully read the passage. What do you note?

Nouns: Capernaum, home, many gathered, no room (even at the door), Jesus, paralytic, four men, roof, faith, child. Verbs: returned, reported, gathered together, preaching, carried, could not get near, removed the roof, made an opening, let down, saw their faith, sins forgiven.

Meditatio—Reflect on the meaning of what you noted during *lectio*.

The crowd gathers because of a report that Jesus is home—why? We don't know why the crowd is there. But what Jesus does is teach—does this imply that what the crowd needs most is truth? The person in great need can't even reach Jesus because of the crowds—they "could not get near." Is there more than the crowd keeping the paralytic far from Jesus? The paralytic only reaches Jesus thanks to his friends. The friends are willing to do whatever it takes—remove the roof, make an opening, let down the pallet—to get the paralyzed man to Jesus. Does faith require such active and persistent work? Jesus sees both the physical and spiritual and addresses the spiritual first. It is a man on the pallet, but Jesus tenderly calls him a "child"—because with the forgiveness of sins he becomes a newborn child of God.

In using my imagination, I might put myself in the place of the friends. It's hard work getting my friend to Jesus, why am I doing it? Or I might put myself in the place of the paralytic: What emotions do I feel for my friends? Am I scared to meet Jesus face to face? What do I think when he first says "your sins are forgiven" and not "walk"? What stirs up in my heart when Jesus addresses me as "child"?

DAY 5 – TRUTH AND BEAUTY

Participants will reflect on Christ in the House of Mary and Martha, *by Alessandro Allori, c. 1578-1580.*

While the gaze of the sisters automatically directs our attention to Jesus, Allori includes several other symbols in his painting that remind us of Christ. What are they?

On the table are loaves of bread and grapes, which allude to Jesus' Real Presence in the Eucharist. Just behind the well, a shepherd walks with a single sheep over his shoulders, reminding us of Jesus' self-description as the Good Shepherd who seeks out the lost sheep. The woman drawing water at the well recalls Jesus' words to the Samaritan woman that he and his gift of the Spirit are living water. If the book in Mary's hands is the Word of God, the Scriptures, then we are reminded of the opening words of St. John's gospel: "In the beginning was the Word, and the Word was with God, and the Word was God" (John 1:1).

NOTES

_____

_____

_____

_____

_____

_____

_____

_____

_____

_____

_____

_____

_____

_____

_____

_____

SESSION 4

ORATIO: CONVERSATION WITH GOD

SESSION OVERVIEW
Read this overview in advance to familiarize yourself with the session.

In the previous session we began to ascend the ladder of *lectio divina* by studying the first two rungs: *lectio*, reading, and *meditatio*, meditation. These first two steps establish the subject matter of prayer with careful reading of and reflection on Scripture.

In this session we move on to the third rung of the ladder, *oratio*. Although this word is often translated as "prayer," a better translation would be "conversing" or "conversation." Often we are tempted to begin with *oratio*, with our own thoughts and words. But Guigo the Carthusian in his ladder of prayer teaches us that if our conversation is to be fruitful, the place to begin ascending the ladder is on the first rungs. Having heard God speak to us in his Word on the first two rungs, we are able to respond on the third rung of *oratio*.

Dr. Gray will spend time looking at St. Augustine as a model of prayer. In his *Confessions*, we see St. Augustine recounting the episodes of his life and understanding them in light of God's Word, just as we are invited to do in *oratio*. From the *Confessions* we also learn that when we do not walk according to God's will and let sin "set up shop" in our lives, we put up barriers that disrupt our prayer. Reconciliation and obedience to God break down these barriers, opening the way for intimate conversation.

Oratio is simply a heart-to-heart conversation with the friend who is "more inward than my innermost self" (St. Augustine), but it still takes practice. This session offers not only the writings of St. Augustine, but also the Lord's Prayer and the Psalms as our guides for growing in our ability to converse deeply with God.

CONNECT

*Begin this session by leading the **Opening Prayer**, and then read or summarize the **Introduction** for your group. Both can be found in the Study Guide.*

*If you have time, review the last session with your group. Can anyone recite the **Memory Verse** (Psalm 84:4-5) without assistance? Otherwise, look it up (page 38) and recite it as a group.*

*Also discuss any highlights or questions the group may have had from the last session's **COMMIT** reflections. Then continue.*

What makes it easy to have a deep, meaningful conversation with a close friend?

Having a close, healthy relationship makes it easier to have a deep conversation. It's often awkward to try to talk about something intimate or important with a friend who we do not know well. It's also helpful to have time and space set aside for the conversation—have it be intentional rather than random. And there must be an actual topic of conversation; it's hard to have a deep conversation about nothing in particular. In this session we will be looking at how to make the most of our time conversing with God in oratio.

Think of a time when you felt distant from a friend and had a hard time talking with that person. What was getting in the way of conversation?

Answers may be very personal. The details aren't necessary, so encourage participants to share their experiences in general, to help them feel comfortable. A disagreement or a fight can put distance in a relationship and make conversation difficult at best, sometimes leading to a complete breakdown in communication. This question sets the stage for understanding how moral barriers that disrupt our relationship with God also become major barriers to conversing with God in prayer. Just as a fight with a friend or spouse makes it hard to talk with him/her easily, so also our sin makes it hard for us to hear and talk to God.

 Play the video segment, which will last about 31 minutes. The Study Guide provides participants with a brief outline of the topics covered in the video teaching, along with the following discussion questions.

DISCUSS

After the video segment, discuss the following questions. Familiarize yourself with the comments after each question; these are meant to guide you in the conversation.

CONVERSATION WITH GOD

1. What was one thing you heard for the first time or that was an "aha" moment for you?

St. Augustine's Confessions *and the model of prayer as a dialogue in that work may be new or particularly striking to some participants. The idea of moral barriers disrupting both our relationship with God and our conversation in prayer make another striking point, as well as the connection between almsgiving, fasting, and fruitful prayer.*

2. What are some examples of moral barriers to prayer (either general or from personal experience)? What are some specific ways to overcome these particular barriers?

Encourage participants to share general examples if they are not comfortable sharing from personal experience. Some examples of moral barriers: addiction to pornography, abuse of alcohol or drugs, sloth (e.g., too great an attachment to sleep), excessive time spent watching TV or playing online games, etc. For any habitual sin or attachment to things of this world that is brought up as an example, participants can find a virtue to help overcome that barrier. Practicing temperance with food, drink, or time spent with technology (or fasting from something to which they are too attached) would be one example. Making a point of getting to Confession would be a great place to start.

3. What is your experience with praying the psalms? What is your favorite psalm? Why?
Encourage those with experience praying the Liturgy of the Hours to talk about that. Others may pray with some favorite psalms or use hymns and songs based on the psalms in their personal prayer. Everyone who attends Mass has experience with praying the Responsorial Psalm during the liturgy. If participants don't have a specific favorite psalm, encourage them to share what type of psalm they prefer—praise, thanksgiving, lament, or happy, sad, in danger, etc.

*Direct participants to this session's **Memory Verse** in their Study Guides, and read it together. Then lead the **Closing Prayer**. Encourage participants to do the **COMMIT** reflections on their own before you meet again as a group.*

COMMIT

*Following are suggested answers to the questions participants will be asked in their daily **COMMIT** reflections.*

DAY 1 – ST. AUGUSTINE: MODEL OF PRAYER
Participants will look at St. Augustine and his Confessions *to find a model of prayer as dialogue and prayer using the words of Scripture.*

What questions does St. Augustine have for God in this passage?
St. Augustine wants to know whether knowledge and understanding of God come first followed by prayer, or whether praying to God comes before knowledge and understanding.

Look up the following verses. What answer does St. Augustine find from God in Scripture?
Romans 10:14 – *We can't pray to God if we don't know him or believe in him. To know and believe in him we must have heard about him from someone. (Prayer requires some level of understanding.)*
Psalm 22:26 & Jeremiah 29:13 – *If we seek God, we will find him and praise him. (Seeking leads us to prayer.)*
St. Augustine finds that the answer is "both." God will reveal himself to all who seek—we can pray (seek) and understanding will follow; but we cannot truly pray to God if we don't know him, so understanding will lead us to better prayer. It is a cycle. Each continually leads to the other.

Try it on your own using the passage from John 5:2–9.
Lectio—Carefully read the passage. What do you note?
The detailed location of this miracle: Jerusalem, Sheep Gate, Bethesda pools. Passage gives detail of the "multitude"—invalids, blind, lame, paralyzed—and notes the "one man." This "sick man" has been "ill" a "long time"—thirty-eight years. Jesus asks the man if he wants to be healed even though his illness is readily apparent and Jesus already knows that he has been there a long time. Jesus gives direct, active instructions to the man—"rise," "take up," "walk." The man was healed "at once."

Meditatio—Reflect on the meaning of what you noted during *lectio.*

The detailed/specific location reminds us that God enters into human history—any first-century Christian could go to the location of this miracle, and even today it is possible to visit the location on a pilgrimage—and God wants to enter into "my" history. The details about the individual ailments of the multitude, and the "one man," remind us that God also knows our exact needs. Jesus asks if the man wants to be healed. He doesn't go against our free will, but rather invites us. Jesus starts the conversation with this question. We might reflect on whether the man's response is an excuse, blaming others, or an honest assessment of his troubles. Even though the passage doesn't record the man's "yes, I want to be healed" or any verbal response to Jesus' question, this man must have responded immediately in his heart because "at once" he is healed.

Oratio—Journal your conversation with God.

The reflections above might lead participants to journal about these types of questions and responses: I thank God for his intimate and personal love for me. I ask God to open my eyes to the things of which I need to be healed. Even though God knows what I need, I still need to ask him for it in prayer. Asking God for what I need helps me become more aware of what my real needs are and reminds me that it is God who meets my needs. Even though I might have had an infirmity or trouble for "a long time," do I still trust that God can heal me? That God loves me? I might take stock of whether God is giving me direction in my life. Am I responding to this direction? Am I responding honestly? Or am I making excuses?

DAY 2 – BARRIERS TO CONVERSATION
Participants reflect on what gets in the way of conversing with God in oratio.

Read Psalm 32. How do we break down the barrier of sin and repair our relationship with God?
In Psalm 32 the psalmist says, "I acknowledged my sin to thee, and I did not hide my iniquity; I said, 'I will confess my transgressions to the LORD'; then thou didst forgive the guilt of my sin" (verse 5), and with forgiveness comes instruction, teaching, and counsel from the Lord.

What attachments might be hindering your *oratio*? What steps can you take this week to cultivate a deeper intimacy with God and break down any moral barriers to prayer?
This is a chance to take a more personal look at what was discussed in general after watching the video. Personal sins, attachments to things that may be good in and of themselves but still distract us from God, or frustration with God over an unanswered prayer or difficult situation—all of these can disrupt our prayer. Confession, time in Adoration, and fasting from something are examples of steps to take to break down these barriers. Simply recognizing and acknowledging the existence of a barrier is an important first step!

Practice *lectio, meditatio,* and *oratio* using the passage from Psalm 139:1–6.
Lectio—Carefully read the passage. What do you note?
Participants might note the primary theme of "knowing": "All my ways" are known—when I sit, when I rise, my path, my lying down. God searches, knows, discerns, is acquainted…knows it "altogether"…and such knowledge is described as "too wonderful."

Meditatio—Reflect on the meaning of what you noted during *lectio.*
Reflections on the careful reading might include: The psalm's repetition and numerous examples emphasize how deeply and intimately God knows me. There is nothing I can hide from God. If God knows a word before I speak it, then he must know me better than I know myself!

Oratio—Journal your conversation with God.

Participants might journal on any of the following: I can't hide anything from God, so I might as well stop trying. If I don't recognize something that is going on in my own heart, I need to ask God to reveal it, because he sees it before I do. God lays his hand upon me...does this bring me comfort, safety? Or is there sin in my life that makes me want to pull away from God's hand? God's intimate knowledge of me is "wonderful"—does this intimacy bring me wonder at how the God of the universe knows me? Or is this maybe intimidating ("too wonderful")?

DAY 3 – LECTIO: LORD, TEACH US TO PRAY

Participants will reflect on Jesus teaching his disciples to pray the Lord's Prayer.

LECTIO

What instructions does Jesus give concerning prayer (place, manner, how we address God, etc.)?
Pray in secret, do not use more words just for the sake of a longer prayer, address God as Father, forgive others so that our prayers for forgiveness will be heard and answered.

Look for the verbs used in the Our Father. What is the first thing we ask for in this prayer? How do the petitions progress? Is there a pattern?
We first ask for God's name to be hallowed (made holy or recognized as holy). The petitions progress from a focus on God in heaven to his kingdom and will being manifest not only in heaven but in us, to provision for us on earth, and to our relationships with others.

What is required of us in order for our prayer for forgiveness to be heard and answered?
We must first forgive others.

MEDITATIO

What is the significance of beginning prayer by addressing God as "our Father"? What does this teach us about prayer in general?
God truly loves us and cares for us—we can trust him to answer our prayer because he is our Father. It also means we approach him in boldness as sons and daughters, rather than as mere servants or slaves.

Which of the petitions of the Lord's Prayer stands out the most to you? Why?
A particular petition may stand out because a person understands it in a new way after the meditation (e.g., understanding why we ask for God's name to be hallowed when he is holy in and of himself without our help), or it may stand out because that need is particularly strong right now (e.g., "thy will be done" because I am struggling to align my will with God's over something in particular).

In Matthew's gospel, the Lord's Prayer is framed by instructions concerning almsgiving (Matthew 6:1–4) and fasting (Matthew 6:16–18). What relationship do these two practices have to prayer? Why are they so important?
We must learn how to live lives of love if we want to have intimate conversation with the God who is Love. Almsgiving and fasting teach us love for neighbor and detachment from self, and they therefore bring us into closer relationship with God, making prayer more intimate and more effective.

DAY 4 – PSALMS: A SCHOOL OF PRAYER

Participants will look at the psalms as a model of prayer as well as a crucial element of the prayer life of the Christian in union with the whole Church.

Read Psalm 28. According to this psalm, how do we avoid wickedness? How do we live righteously?

The wicked "speak peace with their neighbors, while mischief is in their hearts"; they work evil deeds and "do not regard the works of the LORD." So we must be honest in our dealings with others, do good and not evil, be mindful of God and his works, and trust in God as our strength and shield, in order to live righteously.

Look up the following psalms. What is going on in David's life when he writes each psalm?

Psalm 3 – *Written when David had to flee Jerusalem because his son Absalom was leading a coup to take over the throne of David, his father.*

Psalm 51 – *Written after David sinned with Bathsheba.*

Psalm 57 – *Written when David was hiding from Saul because Saul sought his life.*

Now try it on your own using the passage from Psalm 130:1–8.

Lectio—Carefully read the passage. What do you note?

Participants might note any of the following: repetition of the divine name (LORD), repetition of the plea to be heard and forgiven, expression of trust that God will forgive, and comparison of the soul's waiting to the watchman.

Meditatio—Reflect on the meaning of what you noted during *lectio.*

Psalmist doesn't just cry out to God, but cries "out of the depths." The watchman watches for morning, day, and light; he doesn't leave his post until his time is over—just as my soul "watches" and "waits." While the psalmist talks about God being feared, he also speaks of hoping in the Lord and finding mercy and plenteous redemption, so the fear of God is not something that keeps us away, but draws us to God in wonder. Psalmist speaks of "plenteous redemption"—God's mercy is not sparse or limited, but full and abundant; it redeems "all" iniquity.

Oratio—Journal your conversation with God.

Some examples of what participants may journal: I am drawn to heartfelt expression of my contrition, my need for forgiveness, and my trust that God will forgive and heal. I feel anew the truth that God will lift up my soul from the depths of sin to the bright morning of his forgiveness and redemption. I have a new understanding that God can forgive "all" my iniquity. I share with God my joy in a new understanding of the hope I have in his mercy. I challenged to be like a watchman, in the sense that I am on the watch for occasions of sin so as to do better at avoiding them.

DAY 5 – TRUTH AND BEAUTY

Participants will reflect on King David Playing the Harp, Domenichino, c. 1620.

Look up the following verses. How is David described?

1 Samuel 16:16–23 – *David was "skilful in playing" and he "took the lyre and played it with his hand; so Saul was refreshed."*

2 Samuel 6:5 – *David (and all Israel) was making merry with "songs and lyres and harps and tambourines and castanets and cymbals."*

1 Chronicles 16:4–9 – *Not only did David play and sing himself (as seen in the above verses), but when the Ark of the Covenant was finally moved to Jerusalem, he ordained that the Lord's praises should continually be sung before God's presence in the Ark.*

Look at the introductory line of the first ten psalms. How many are attributed to David?
Seven of the first ten psalms are attributed to David.

NOTES

_____

_____

_____

_____

_____

_____

_____

_____

_____

_____

_____

_____

_____

_____

SESSION 5

CONTEMPLATIO: THE GAZE OF LOVE

SESSION OVERVIEW

Read this overview in advance to familiarize yourself with the session.

We have examined the way in which climbing the ladder of prayer requires us to use the full powers of our minds and hearts to read, reflect, and respond in *lectio*, *meditatio*, and *oratio*. Although God always initiates the encounter of prayer, success in climbing these first three rungs of the ladder is also dependent on the effort we put forth.

The fourth rung of the ladder is entirely different. In *contemplatio* we cease to be the ones acting in prayer and we simply receive the gift of contemplation God offers to us. This encounter with God is very difficult to define or explain. Instead, contemplation is most often described using analogies—tasting, seeing, etc.—showing rather than explaining or defining. One way to describe *contemplatio* is as a gaze of love: we gaze upon Love himself and rest in his loving embrace.

Whether fleeting moments or extended periods of time in the presence of the Beloved, these encounters are to be remembered. God's people remembered their encounters with God in the Torah, and celebrated them in their annual feasts. We do this remembering of special encounters in our temporal life when we celebrate anniversaries and birthdays, when we take pictures of favorite vacations or trips. In our spiritual life we too need to remember our encounters with God, these pearls of great price, so that when trial and dryness arise in our prayer and our life, we can recall God's love and remember Love's presence even in the midst of what appears to be his absence.

Contemplatio is the pinnacle of the ladder of prayer. We begin by seeking the face of God, like Moses on Mount Sinai, and David in Psalm 27:8. After the arduous work of ascent, we rest in the peace of this supernatural encounter with God. The key to *contemplatio* is love—in seeking God's face, we must also seek to love ever more perfectly in order to be prepared to receive and return this gaze of God's perfect love.

CONNECT

*Begin this session by leading the **Opening Prayer** and reading aloud the **Introduction**, both found in the Study Guide.*

*If you have time, review the last session with your group. Can anyone recite the **Memory Verse** (Luke 11:1) without assistance? Otherwise, look it up (page 56) and recite it as a group.*

*Also discuss any highlights or questions the group may have had from the last session's **COMMIT** reflections. Then continue.*

Describe a time when you were completely caught up in gazing at someone you love or something you thought was beautiful. What did you feel in that moment? Is what you felt easy to describe?
Some examples may include seeing your spouse on your wedding day, watching your child sleep, or meeting up with a dear friend after a long absence. Other examples could include being lost in wonder at a beautiful sunrise, a majestic mountain view, or a magnificent work of art. These moments, while they mark our heart and memory in profound ways, are often hard to put into words. Contemplatio is a gaze of love exchanged with God—we can begin to describe this in terms of how we experience a "gaze of love" in human relationships and the natural world.

What is something that you really want but can't work for or achieve on your own? Think of something you can prepare for but have to wait to receive from someone else.
We prepare ourselves to be properly disposed to receive the gift of contemplation, but it is not something we can make happen on our own—it is a gift from God. Some other gifts we can prepare for but not make happen by our own effort might include maintaining good health (to do everything right, but having to wait patiently for healing), having children, waiting for a vocation to be revealed, waiting for a marriage proposal, etc.

Play the video segment, which will last about 28 minutes. The Study Guide provides participants with a brief outline of the topics covered in the video teaching, along with the following discussion questions.

DISCUSS

After the video segment, discuss the following questions. Familiarize yourself with the comments after each question; these are meant to guide you in the conversation.

THE GAZE OF LOVE

1. What was one thing you heard for the first time or that was an "aha" moment for you?
Some new or particularly striking ideas may include the description of contemplation in terms of tasting or seeing, the fact that contemplation is a gift and not something we can achieve if we just try hard enough, Blaise Pascal's description of his encounter with God, etc.

2. What do you think it means to look at God and have him look at you, and for that to be "enough," as the man in St. John Vianney's parish described?
One possible answer: The idea of looking at God and being looked at by him is an encounter of simply being present—you don't have to say anything or figure anything out; it is just an awareness of God's love for you and your love for God. It is peaceful and restful, not demanding. An analogous experience might be a couple married many years who are happy just being together with no need to speak.

3. Why is it so important to remember our encounters with God, both personally (like Pascal) and communally (like Israel)? How do you do this?

Scripture sets the example for remembering and celebrating our encounters with God. The memory can sustain and encourage us through difficult times. Remembering God's encounters with his people communally (as a Church, as Israel did) builds faith and a sense of community. Some people may use words to remember (like Pascal's note), while others may use art or music to commemorate the encounter. Journaling about our prayer time is a wonderful way to keep an ongoing remembrance of our encounters with God in prayer—both the words and direction we receive in lectio/meditation/oratio, *and also any encounters of* contemplatio.

*Direct participants to this session's **Memory Verse** in their Study Guides, and read it together. Then lead the **Closing Prayer**. Encourage participants to do the **COMMIT** reflections on their own before you meet again as a group.*

COMMIT

*Following are suggested answers to the questions participants will be asked in their daily **COMMIT** reflections.*

DAY 1 – CONTEMPLATION: THE GAZE AND FRUIT OF LOVE
Participants will explore contemplation as a gaze of love and the fruit of the labor of lectio/mediatio/oratio.

What can you do to increase your love and virtue and make yourself ready for *contemplatio*? Where do you feel your efforts stop and God's gift begins?

Anything we do to deepen our love for God helps prepare us to receive the gift of contemplation. Some specific examples would be to go to Confession, to work to root out sin in our lives, and to love those around us more perfectly. We should especially prepare for contemplation by working diligently and faithfully at prayer through lectio, meditatio, *and* oratio. *There may not be a clearly perceived line between our own efforts and God's gift because prayer is itself a gift that requires our effort in response. God initiates, we work at it, and sometimes we also receive the gift of true contemplation. All of our hard work should serve to remind us that it is God who works first and who works in and through us even in our work.*

Spend some time in *lectio divina* today reflecting on God's love and his invitation to "come away" in the passage from Song of Solomon 2:10–13.
Lectio—Carefully read the passage. What do you note?
The bride (my soul) is twice described using the words "my love" and "my fair one." Images of springtime include flowers, blossoms, fragrance, birds, new birth/growth, freshness, fruit, a sense of readiness and anticipation, but also pruning. The call from the Bridegroom (Christ) is to "arise" and "come away."

Meditatio—Reflect on the meaning of what you noted during *lectio*.
This is an invitation to an intimate encounter with the Beloved. The time of sitting and waiting is over, and we are called to "arise" and "come." The signs of spring alert our senses—sight (seeing flowers), smell (smelling the fragrances), and taste (anticipating the figs of the tree and the wine from the vines).

Oratio—Journal your conversation with God.

My Beloved is calling me—will I respond? Will I arise eagerly and go, or will I hesitate? Why do I hesitate? Is it out of fear? Pride? Distrust? Is there pruning needed for a more fruitful harvest in my soul? Do I recognize that everything in the passage (signs of spring, etc.) point me to my Beloved? Do I see these same signs in my day-to-day life? Where? Give God thanks for the many signs of his love.

Contemplatio—Take time to simply rest in God's presence.

DAY 2 – ADORATION: AN ENCOUNTER OF THE BELOVED

Participants will reflect on how Adoration of the Blessed Sacrament helps us practice and prepare for an experience of contemplation.

When is the last time you went to an adoration chapel? Or stopped by a church to visit our Lord in the tabernacle? What was your experience of prayer during that time?

Some participants may not have much experience at all with Adoration; others might make a regular Holy Hour. Anyone who has experienced Adoration multiple times is likely to have had a wide range of experiences—from initial distraction due to the quiet, to deep, fruitful prayer.

Make time this week to visit our Lord in the tabernacle or adoration chapel, and, as you join the Beloved Disciple close to Christ's heart, practice the "art of prayer" using the passage from Psalm 24:3–6.

Lectio—Carefully read the passage. What do you note?

Themes include: purity/worthiness—clean hands, pure heart; seeking God's face, seeking his dwelling ascending, standing, lifting up; and God described as Lord, God of Jacob, and God of [my] salvation.

Meditatio—Reflect on the meaning of what you noted during *lectio*.

Themes of purity and worthiness are contrasted to what is "false" and deceitful…these are two different options/paths, and we must choose one. If we strive to be worthy and "seek" God faithfully, then we will receive blessing, vindication, and "see" God, and not only see but also "stand" in his presence. Who stands in the presence of a king? God is personal, he is Lord, he is Jacob's God.

Oratio—Journal your conversation with God.

How do I prepare myself for an encounter with God? Do I go into it aware of my sin and my need for forgiveness? How do I approach God with clean hands and a pure heart? Are there false things to which I lift up my soul instead of to God? Is God, "my" God, the God of "my salvation," lord of my life, my whole life? Can I put my name in the place of Jacob: the God of _____? How much effort do I put into seeking his face? How can I seek him more diligently? How do I feel God drawing me upward, toward himself?

Contemplatio—Take time to simply rest in God's presence.

DAY 3 – LECTIO: ELIJAH AND THE STILL SMALL VOICE

Participants will reflect on Elijah fleeing from Jezebel and encountering God at Mount Horeb.

LECTIO

What is God's question for Elijah? Look at 1 Kings 19:7–8. Why is this question unexpected?

God asks Elijah, "What are you doing here?" In verses 7-8 it is the angel of the Lord who speaks of "the journey," so it is God who directed Elijah to Mount Horeb.

How is the voice of God's presence described? What adjectives are used? Look up the definitions for these words.

God's presence is described as a "still small voice."

Still – remaining in place, at rest; free from sound or noise; subdued or low in sound; free from turbulence or commotion; peaceful; tranquil.

Small – of limited size, not big, little; not great in amount, degree, extent, duration, value, etc.

What is the major repetition in this passage? What is framed by the repetition?

God asks Elijah, "What are you doing here?" Elijah repeats that he has been jealous for the Lord, the God of hosts, and faithful to the Lord, while Israel has forsaken God—that he is the only faithful one left, and his life is in danger because of it. God responds with "Go"—first directing Elijah for his encounter on the mountain, and then directing him to his next mission.

This repetition of Elijah's faithfulness and his despair (because he appears to be the only faithful one) frames his encounter with God in the still small voice.

MEDITATIO

Elijah's joy at following God no matter the consequences has been lost, and instead there is despair. How does God put Elijah back on track?

Most of us have probably felt overwhelmed by what God is asking of us at some point, even if we haven't felt specifically that the benefits don't match up to the cost. If we pay attention, God puts the same question to us as he did to Elijah: "What are you doing here?" It's a time for us to step back and reflect on whether our focus is still on God, or on us. Is our faithfulness because of love, personal love of God? God puts Elijah back on track with a personal, profound encounter with himself. When discouragement and despair come, we too need to return to God in a deeper way and meet him in Scripture and spiritual reading as well as in friends or mentors, so that we return to the joy we can only find in God.

Once Elijah recognizes God's presence, what does he do? Why?

When Elijah hears the still small voice and recognizes God's presence, "He wrapped his face in his mantle and went out and stood at the entrance of the cave." Elijah recognizes the God whom he loves and cannot remain in the cave. In humility he covers his face before the God of heaven, but he "went out"—to be as close as possible to the Lord.

What does it mean that Elijah is "jealous" for the Lord? How do his jealously and faithfulness open the door to his encounter with God at Mount Horeb? What does the framing of Elijah's encounter with the repetition noted above teach us?

Elijah recognizes that worship belongs rightfully to God alone, and he wants God to have what is his—he doesn't want Israel to chase after false idols. Even in the midst of his despair, Elijah is a man who seeks God diligently and loves God faithfully, and this prepares him for the encounter at Horeb. If he did not already love God and desire God, he would not be so quick to recognize God. You have to be listening already to hear the still small voice. The repetition reminds us of this, and also that God sends us out to witness to him—"Go"—but that mission always starts, and re-starts, with our personal encounter with God.

DAY 4 – REMEMBERING THE ENCOUNTER WITH GOD
Participants will examine the importance of remembering and celebrating our encounters with God.

What are some ways you remember and celebrate important moments of your life?
Some examples are journaling, pictures, birthday parties, blog posts, anniversary celebrations, etc.

Read Psalm 77. How does calling to mind Israel's past encounters with God shape the psalmist's prayer?
The psalmist has an idea of what God should do because he remembers what God has done. His perception is that God has changed—in the past he rescued Israel, but now he seems distant (this is his emotion/perception, not a claim that God does change). But instead of despairing, the psalmist chooses to "call to mind the deeds of the LORD" (v. 11), and so his prayer of sorrow and lament turns to a prayer of praise as he recalls Israel's encounters with God in the past and is renewed in his trust that Israel will again encounter God in his mighty power.

Spend some time in *lectio divina* today, joining the psalmist and his exhortation to "remember the works" of the Lord using a passage from Psalm 105:1–6.

Lectio—Carefully read the passage. What do you note?
Psalmist uses strong action verbs in his exhortation—give thanks, call on, make known, sing, sing praises, tell, glory, seek, remember. Notice the object of all these actions—either it is God (i.e., it is the Lord/his name that receives our thanks, calling, singing, glory) or it is his actions (i.e., it is the Lord's deeds/works/miracles/judgments that are to be told of, made known, or remembered).

Meditatio—Reflect on the meaning of what you noted during *lectio.*
In order to give thanks/make known/sing of God's deeds, we must first remember them. But remembering should then lead to thanking/praising/singing/glorying in God. Part of remembering is telling others what God has done. All of this leads to seeking God yet again—one encounter leads to another. Identity is in terms of encounter (we are "offspring" of "Abraham his servant" and his "chosen ones").

Oratio—Journal your conversation with God.
Talk with God about the deeds and works that I remember. To what does my remembering lead? Am I led to praise and give thanks? Am I led to singing and giving glory to my Lord? Am I led closer again to God by remembering previous encounters with him? When I call to mind God's gaze of love, does it lead me to share his love with others?

Contemplatio—Take time to simply rest in God's presence.

DAY 5 – TRUTH AND BEAUTY
Participants will reflect on St. Augustine and his mother St. Monica, Ary Scheffer, c. 1846, Louvre Museum, Paris.

(No questions this Commit Day.)

SESSION 6

RESOLUTIO: PUTTING LOVE INTO ACTION

SESSION OVERVIEW

Read this overview in advance to familiarize yourself with the session.

In the last session we examined the fourth rung of Guigo's ladder, *contemplatio*. Unlike the earlier rungs, *contemplatio* is not something we achieve simply by our own efforts. We prepare carefully in order to properly dispose ourselves for it, but this "gaze of love" is completely God's gift.

Dr. Gray will begin this last session with a beautiful image/analogy of the vineyard of *lectio divina*. *Lectio* is like plucking the grapes in the vineyard—we read carefully and pluck the words and images from the vine of the text. *Meditatio* is like squeezing the juice out of the grape—peering more deeply into what we have read, we see and understand more clearly its meaning. *Oratio* is like the fermentation period—our conversation bubbles up from our *lectio* and *meditatio*. *Contemplatio* is the last step, where we enjoy the aged, fine wine in our *lectio*, *meditatio*, and *oratio*; this step takes time, but is worth the wait. Dr. Gray reminds us that sometimes we are tempted to stop at meditation, but if we do this, then according to this analogy, we can only drink grape juice. *Lectio* and *meditatio* are to lead us to the more intimate encounters of *oratio* and *contemplatio*.

The four traditional steps of *lectio divina* lead naturally to a fifth step: *resolutio*, the resolution to put our prayer into action. Following *contemplatio*, the peaceful rest in God's loving gaze, *resolutio* allows God to teach us how to extend that gaze of love to our neighbor. Without resolution and action, prayer runs the risk of increasing our pride rather than our virtue, as St. Francis de Sales and other great saints so clearly remind and exhort. After encountering the God of Love in the dialogue of prayer, we must take action to allow God's love to transform our lives. While making a resolution and putting it into practice sounds straightforward, it can often prove the most difficult part of prayer. For this reason, our resolutions should not be general goals, but small, particular actions so that we can make and measure our progress.

Dr. Gray closes this last session with some practical notes for making *lectio divina* part of our prayer lives. The Church gives us a ready-made plan in the Mass and its daily readings, as well as the Liturgy of the Hours. Any of the books of the Bible can be used, but especially the psalms and the gospels, both of which the Church puts before us in her liturgy each day.

CONNECT

*Begin this session by leading the **Opening Prayer**, and then read or summarize the **Introduction** for your group. Both can be found in the Study Guide.*

*If you have time, review the last session with your group. Can anyone recite the **Memory Verse** (Psalm 27:8) without assistance? Otherwise, look it up (page 74) and recite it as a group.*

*Also discuss any highlights or questions the group may have had from the last session's **COMMIT** reflections. Then continue.*

Do you think there are any risks or potential dangers associated with prayer? What might they be?
Most of us probably don't think of prayer as being risky or dangerous—but if our prayer is not what it is supposed to be and we don't realize that, then we will fall into a trap of empty, unproductive prayer. In this session we will examine a quote from St. Francis de Sales, warning that prayer that does not lead to action runs the risk of puffing us up with pride.

Do you find it easier to keep broad, sweeping resolutions (e.g., "Be a better person") or smaller, specific resolutions (e.g., "Make my bed first thing every morning")? Why?
It is typically easier to follow through on a small, specific resolution. We don't lose sight of the goal in trying to figure out a strategy to accomplish it because the plan for action is obvious when the resolution is specific. If we aim too broad, we often get mired down in all the options for how and where to start, and all too often we either never start, or we start and then quit due to discouragement at the slow rate of progress. Resolutio in prayer should be small and practical in order to be fruitful.

 Play the video segment, which will last about 31 minutes. The Study Guide provides participants with a brief outline of the topics covered in the video teaching, along with the following discussion questions.

DISCUSS

After the video segment, discuss the following questions. Familiarize yourself with the comments after each question; these are meant to guide you in the conversation.

PUTTING LOVE INTO ACTION

1. What was one thing you heard for the first time or that was an "aha" moment for you?
Some new or remarkable ideas may include: the process of wine-making as a metaphor or analogy for prayer, that prayer can make us like the Pharisees if we don't put it into action, or prayer not being an end in itself but rather a means to an end.

2. Why is it so important to put prayer into action? What do you think would happen to a prayer life that didn't regularly include *resolutio*?
Meditating on God's Word, on truth and holiness, is wonderful. But without action, we can easily deceive ourselves that we are just as good and holy as what we read, without the reality existing in our lives. This could lead to complacency, pride, etc. If our prayer life is to bear abundant fruit, we need to make a concrete resolution each day and then follow through and act on that resolution.

3. What is your favorite reading material to use for prayer? Why?
Lectio divina might still be new enough to some participants that they don't have a favorite resource yet. Others may prefer the psalms or the gospels, as Dr. Gray recommends. Some participants may already be in the habit of praying all or part of the Liturgy of the Hours and using that for lectio; others may attend daily Mass or regularly read the daily readings for prayer. This is a good time for participants to share favorite resources such as Magnificat, websites, or apps to help with prayer such as iBreviary, Divine Office, Laudate, etc.

*Direct participants to this session's **Memory Verse** in their Study Guides, and read it together. Then lead the **Closing Prayer**. Encourage participants to do the **COMMIT** reflections on their own before you meet again as a group.*

COMMIT

*Following are suggested answers to the questions participants will be asked in their daily **COMMIT** reflections.*

DAY 1 – IMPORTANCE OF A RESOLUTION

Participants will look at why resolutio *is so important to prayer and what St. Francis de Sales warns about prayer without action in his* Introduction to the Devout Life.

What does our Lord's model of prayer in Gethsemane teach us about the importance of *resolutio*?
Jesus shows us how to submit our will to God's. In his prayer we find permission to not want to suffer, but we also find strength and encouragement for choosing to accept whatever God wills. Jesus makes his submission to the Father's will explicit in his resolutio: *"Not as I will, but as you will." This shows us that we shouldn't just give an easy and quick general resolution, but rather we should make our submission clear and specific, in order that we may be strengthened by God's grace for the specific work ahead.*

Spend some time in *lectio divina* today reflecting on St. James' exhortation to put our prayer into action using the passage from James 1:19–25.
Lectio—Carefully read the passage. What do you note?
Quick to hear versus slow to speak or anger. Sin is described "ugly" words, such as "filthiness" and "rank growth." God's Word is described as "implanted." Repetition of "hearer" and "doer." Image of face in a mirror. Law, described with "perfect" and "of liberty." "Doer/doing" strengthened with "perseveres." We must also act—to obey. To hear is to obey/do and then to be blessed.

Meditatio—Reflect on the meaning of what you noted during *lectio*.
We should listen more ("be quick") than we talk ("be slow")—especially in prayer, but also in our relationships with others. How is the "anger of man" in opposition to the "righteousness of God"? Rather than "growth of wickedness," it is the "implanted word" that needs to grow in me, and if I let this grow it can "save my soul." If we are attached to sin, we won't be able to hear God in prayer, and his Word won't be active in our souls. To hear without doing is to not perceive reality clearly (see in a mirror and then forget immediately).

Oratio—Journal your conversation with God.
How much do I listen? Does my pride make me want to do all the talking and take center stage? Bring to God any relationships that I need to reorder. In prayer, am I afraid to be quiet and wait for God's direction? I might share with God my current struggles in prayer. How many times has my anger worked against God's will or God's love for me and for others? What sins have I chosen to not see as they truly are—filthy and rank? Ask God to open my eyes to new ways he wants me to reform my life with his grace. What do I "hear" God directing me to "do"? Reflect on how God's laws and ways, his perfect law, offers liberty, freedom, and peace in my life.

Contemplatio—Take time to simply rest in God's presence.

Resolutio—What small thing can you do today to put your prayer into action?
I might make a resolution to listen to a particular friend more diligently. I might resolve to make my first words in conversation those of a question or two, which allows the other person to speak. I might resolve to go to Confession as a result of God opening my eyes to a particular sin. I might resolve to study Scripture more purposely so that I can more diligently "look into" God's "perfect law."

DAY 2 – ACTION AS THE FRUIT OF PRAYER

Participants will reflect on how action flows naturally out of prayer and how St. Teresa of Avila describes prayer as ordered toward works of service.

If prayer is a means to an end, does that make it more or less important? Why?

As important and essential as prayer is, it is not the most important thing, in as much as it is not the "end" or ultimate goal. But this does not mean that prayer is not important; in fact, if we are to obtain the ultimate goal of love—love of God and love of neighbor—prayer is vital. The goal of love makes prayer that much more important because in spending time with Love himself in prayer, we learn better just how to love and are strengthened to act in love.

Look up James 2:14–26. How does the relationship between faith and works, as described by St. James, shed light on the relationship between prayer and action?

Faith without works is dead, and prayer without action is empty or dead as well. The relationship is very similar. We can be tempted to see both faith and prayer as something mental/interior, and to separate them from exterior action—but this is a great error, as both faith and prayer must lead to action.

Spend some time in *lectio divina* today reflecting on how Jesus himself emphasizes the importance of action as the fruit of our prayer using the passage from Matthew 25:31–40.

Lectio—Carefully read the passage. What do you note?

A table of acacia wood overlaid with pure gold, with rings and poles by which it was to be carried. Plates, dishes, flagons, and bowls all made of gold to be used on the table. Twelve cakes of bread were put on the table in two rows of six.

Meditatio—Reflect on the meaning of what you noted during *lectio*.

Note the time of what is described: the end times. Gathering versus separating. Jesus is not named but described as Son of man and King. Repetition of the list of works of mercy. Pattern of need followed by action. Those who are righteous act, they did these things. The king speaks of "my brethren." The righteous on Jesus' right repeatedly ask "when?"

Oratio—Journal your conversation with God.

Do I see Jesus Christ as the King of my life? King of my actions? Do I see Christ in others? Do I see others as the brothers and sisters of Christ (his "brethren" as Jesus calls them)? Do I see others as "my" brothers and sisters in Christ? Am I willing to love others, even if I might not "like" them at the moment? Where do I see these needs described by Jesus around me—friends, children, co-workers, the poor? Am I already doing some of these works of mercy regularly? Am I doing these works with true love and charity? Which can I do more diligently? If I am not doing any of these works, what is God calling me to?

Contemplatio—Take time to simply rest in God's presence.

Resolutio—What small thing can you do today to put your prayer into action?

A few ideas: I might resolve to do one work of mercy mentioned in the gospel passage today or this week. I might recognize the humility of the righteous and resolve to grow in humility by doing one kind act anonymously today.

DAY 3 – LECTIO: OVER ALL THESE PUT ON LOVE

Participants will reflect on St. Paul's exhortation to the Colossians to put to death what is earthly and fix their minds on what is of Christ.

LECTIO

What does St. Paul contrast in the first section of this passage (verses 1-5)?
Participants may note the following: Dying/death and being raised/having life with Christ, the things that are above and the things on earth.

What are we to take off or get rid of ("put to death"), and what are we to "put on"?
Get rid of anything earthly: fornication, impurity, passion, evil desire, covetousness, idolatry, anger, wrath, malice, slander, foul talk, lying, and division.
Put on: compassion, kindness, lowliness, meekness, patience, forbearing, forgiveness, and love. Let peace rule your heart, let God's Word dwell in you, and have thankfulness in your hearts.

In the last section of this passage there is a repetition of the command "let" (verses 15 and 16). What are we to let Christ give us? What are these two gifts supposed to accomplish in us?
Let the peace of Christ rule in our hearts, and let the word of Christ dwell richly in us. Together Christ's word and his peace lead us to do all things in his name for the glory of (giving thanks to) God the Father.

MEDITATIO

What is the relationship between the "peace of Christ" (verse 15) and the "word of Christ" (verse 16)? How does this passage encourage us in both contemplative prayer and active love?
Peace is experienced internally, like contemplative prayer, but it will have an outward effect (also like prayer). The word of Christ is related in this passage to teaching and worship—it is more like active prayer/love. Contemplative prayer leads to active love. These two are brought together in the last verse, where "whatever you do, in word or deed" (action) is to be united with "giving thanks to the Father through [Jesus]" (prayer).

What does it mean to "do everything in the name of the Lord Jesus" (verse 17)?
Always be mindful of Jesus, do everything prayerfully, remember that we do everything by God's grace and not our own power, be aware that we are ambassadors of Christ acting in his name, strive to do only his will, etc.

St. Paul gives a very similar exhortation in Ephesians 4:25–5:1, ending with "Therefore be imitators of God, as beloved children." What specific things does St. Paul expect us to do in imitation of God? How does prayer prepare us to be imitators of God?
Some specific expectations are forgiving others, speaking the truth, having patience, showing kindness and compassion, etc. These are all ways that we show our love for God by treating one another in accord with God's will. We cannot imitate God if we do not know him (set our minds on him), and we cannot know him without encountering him in prayer.

DAY 4 – PARTICULAR VS. GENERAL

Participants will examine the importance of forming a small, particular resolution.

Is there someone in your life that is difficult to love, or a situation where you find it especially challenging to serve others? What causes this difficulty?

There might be someone we find somewhat annoying, like in the anecdote Dr. Gray shared about St. Therese of Lisieux and the sister who got on her nerves. Or it might be someone who has hurt us and we have difficulty loving him or her in spite of the hurt. Or we may be struggling with a particular way we are called to love and serve others—cleaning up after kids, an unenjoyable task at work, etc. Although we may initially focus on the situation or the other person as being the source of the difficulty in love, the deepest difficulty lies in our own pride and imperfect love.

Consider some of the following resolutions that might flow from prayer. How are the particular resolutions more practical than the general ones? Complete the chart by providing examples of specific resolutions to replace the general ones.

General Resolution	Particular Resolution
I will be kind to strangers.	I will smile at and try to make eye contact with each person I see today.
I will be more considerate of others' time.	I will be on time for my appointments today.
I will be more generous with my time.	I will read two bedtime stories to my child instead of rushing through one.
I will not be wasteful.	*I will take smaller portions of food and not throw any food away today.*
I will be more forgiving.	*I will choose to forgive my friend/co-worker/spouse for this specific wrong which still bothers me.*
I will be patient.	*I will respond with a charitable tone of voice in a difficult conversation.*
I will take better care of myself.	*I will go to bed at 10pm tonight.*

Spend some time in *lectio divina* today reflecting on St. John's exhortation to love one another using the passage from 1 John 4:7–12, 20–21.

Lectio—Carefully read the passage. What do you note?
Reader addressed as "beloved" and repeated. Repetition of "love," "God," "one another," "brother." Loving related to being "born of God" and "knowing God." Strong verbs: "manifest," "sent," "loved," "abides," "perfected," "seen"...several repeated. Passage ends with "this commandment."

Meditatio—Reflect on the meaning of what you noted during *lectio*.
St. John's address of his reader as "beloved" models the love he is preaching. Use of "only" to describe the Son reminds us of the story of the sacrifice of Isaac, and how much Abraham loved Isaac, and the more perfect love of God the Father for the Son. God the Father "manifests" his love in action (sending the Son). Is "not loving my brother" being equated to "hating my brother"? Loving my brother is a commandment, not just a nice idea.

Oratio—Journal your conversation with God.
I might thank God that he sees me as "beloved." Recalling that God sees my brothers and sisters as "beloved" also, I reflect that it is truly not an option to ignore the call to love my neighbor as myself. I might sense God challenging me, asking me "How seriously do I take loving my brother?" I might be directed to reflect that the two greatest commandments cannot be separated: If I do not love my neighbor then that is proof that I do not love God. Why do I try to love God without trying to love my neighbor better? I might talk with God about specific brothers and sisters. God the Father "manifested" his love in action (sending the Son); I might reflect on how I can better manifest my love for God.

Contemplatio—Take time to simply rest in God's presence.

Resolutio—What small thing can you do today to put your prayer into action?
Offer ideas such as the following: I might resolve to do a specific act of kindness for someone, like writing a short note, letter, or card.

COMMIT DAY 5 – TRUTH AND BEAUTY

Participants will reflect on Clothing the Naked, Works of Mercy—Giving Drink to the Thirsty and Food to the Hungry, *and* Visiting the Sick, *Domenico Ghirlandaio, three of several frescoes in the Oratory of San Martino dei Buonomini, Florence, Italy.*

Look up Matthew 25:31–46. What are the works of mercy that Jesus describes?
Jesus notes the following, beginning in verse 35: feeding the hungry, giving drink to the thirsty, giving shelter to the homeless (i.e. welcoming the stranger), clothing the naked, visiting/caring for the sick, visiting prisoners. Along with these six, the Church also includes burying the dead, which is specifically mentioned in the Old Testament Book of Tobit (see Tobit 1:16–17). Along with these "corporeal" works of mercy, the Church also notes seven additional "spiritual" works of mercy, which include: instructing the ignorant, counseling the doubtful, admonishing sinners, bearing wrongs patiently, forgiving offences willingly, comforting the afflicted, and praying for the living and the dead.

Peter: The Cornerstone of Catholicism

**Was he a poor fisherman? An impetuous student?
A bungling disciple? A coward who became the "Rock"
of the Church?**

Let's find out the answers together with *Lectio: Peter, The Cornerstone of Catholicism*. Ten sessions explore the life of Peter and his relevance to our lives using video and personal study guides.

Presented by Dr. Tim Gray

Dr. Tim Gray is a popular speaker and teacher from the Augustine Institute, renowned for using the Bible, History, and Sacred Tradition and Art to present a fresh perspective on the Catholic Faith.

Sessions Include:

- Put Out Into the Deep: The Making of an Apostle
- Capernaum: Village of Coming Consolation
- Faith Not Fear: Walking in Trust
- Peter the Rock: The Primacy of Jesus
- Peter and the Keys: The Primacy of the Church
- In the Shadow of the Galilean: Peter's Rising Leadership
- Discipleship at a Distance: Peter and the Passion of Christ
- Peter and Pentecost: The Transforming Power of the Holy Spirit
- Peter bar Jonah: How Peter Came to Rome
- *Quo Vadis?:* Peter's Way of the Cross

AUGUSTINE INSTITUTE

Eucharist: Discovering the Mass in the Bible

Jesus said, "This is my Body," and, "This is my Blood."

Some say they're merely symbols of remembrance. Others say they're really the Body and Blood of Christ but can't explain how that's possible. The Eucharist is the center-point of the Mass – but why?

Acclaimed author and scholar Dr. Brant Pitre will tackle those questions and more in *Lectio: Eucharist, Discovering the Mass in the Bible*. In ten sessions, he will open Scripture to deepen our understanding of the mystery and wonder that is the Eucharist—and how it will transform your life.

Sessions Include:

▶ Source & Summit: Introducing the Eucharist

▶ In the Beginning: From the Garden of Eden to Melchizedek

▶ Lamb of God: The Sacrifice of Isaac and the Passover

▶ Manna from Heaven: Miracles of the Exodus

▶ Bread of the Presence: Mysteries of the Tabernacle

▶ Miracles of Jesus: The Wine of Cana and the Loaves and Fishes

▶ Bread of Life: John 6 and the Real Presence

▶ The Last Supper and the Cross: The New Passover of Christ

▶ After the Resurrection: The Road to Emmaus and the Lord's Supper

▶ The Book of Revelation: The Heavenly Worship and the End of Time